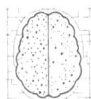

# THE
# NOVEL
# MATRIX

# THE
# NOVEL
# MATRIX

The Complete Novel Writing Guide

## BRAD PAUQUETTE

**BELLWETHER**
SINCE 2009

Cover Designer: Jessica Ostrander
Editorial Team: Rebekah Olson & Thirzah

Print ISBN: 978-1-960230-08-9
Ebook ISBN: 978-1-960230-07-2

Printed in the United States of America
1 3 5 7 9 10 8 6 4 2

# CONTENTS

To Melissa,
who helps me live the best story.

Throughout this book, you'll find QR codes which link to additional resources. These links are included for your benefit.

These QR codes link to the following sites, and the links are safe:
NovelMatrix.com
BradPauquette.com
YouTube.com

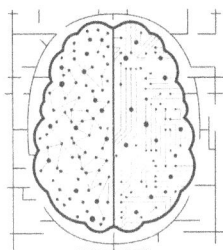

# PROLOGUE

MOST ASPIRING AUTHORS spend hundreds of hours laboring away at books that will never be finished. Even if they're finished, so many of those books won't ever be published or reach any measure of success.

Maybe you're like me, and you already know what it feels like to work and work on a writing project, only to get to the end and find out that the story just doesn't work. So many hours wasted. Is that the game? We just keep rolling the dice until we get lucky enough to land on something good? What if there's a better way?

The problem is simple. It's not bad ideas or even bad writing. The problem is that we're trying to produce something before we take the time to really understand what it is. We all think that just because we've read a lot of books and loved some of them, we ought to be able to sit down and do the same thing.

Maybe some people can. Maybe they get lucky. Maybe they're some kind of story savant.

But if you're anything like me, you have to take the time to understand what you're doing before you can hope to spontaneously achieve it.

1

This is important, because I believe that you have important things to say. Right now, your important messages are getting boggled up, and it's not fair. It's not fair to you that your message gets boggled when there's a solution that can help.

The world needs your ideas. Story is a vehicle for you to change the world.

I've helped hundreds of authors to understand story, and many of them have gone on to win awards and reach best-seller status. If I can help you do the same thing, then the important things you have to say can reach the audience that God is calling you to speak to.

You can change the world. Story is the vehicle. Together, using what I call the *Novel Matrix*, we're going to build a vehicle that works.

Harriet Beecher Stowe wrote *Uncle Tom's Cabin* and changed the world, galvanizing the abolitionist movement and in very real ways sparking the American Civil War. Years later when she met Abraham Lincoln, he reportedly said to her, "So you're the little woman who wrote the book that started this great war."

Upton Sinclair, John Steinbeck, Anne Frank, George Orwell, C. S. Lewis, Isaac Asimov, Frank Peretti...the list goes on—all authors who have changed the way we understand our lives, using fictional stories as the vehicle. Fiction holds the power to change the world—books written by people like you.

You have to change the world. That's what writers do.

I want the world to change. That's why I want you to have these tools.

I first taught a woefully underdeveloped version of this concept at the Columbus Idea Foundry in 2012. It was a six-month course and I think it cost $100.

Over the years, I've had the pleasure of teaching this again and again, connecting with my students and improving it each time.

The purpose of this book is to give you practical instruction for organizing and executing a novel manuscript. I've done my best to stick rigidly to that mission, and to keep the content streamlined and on target.

You can use this book by itself, but it's best used in conjunction with the Novel Matrix classes offered through The Company (visit NovelMatrix.com or Writers.Company). The principles presented here are universal and can be used by anyone, but this book will have a decidedly Christian bent in the examples that are used. I'm a decidedly Christian person and that's just what comes out when I talk.

This book, by itself, will not improve your prose technique or fluency. While you will find some tips for best writing practices sprinkled in, this is a book about story structure. I've written it specifically to help you develop and organize a long-form narrative work.

For our purposes here, a novel is a narrative work of at least 50,000 words. The story can be true or fictional, as long as it's organized like a story. Non-fiction books of an informational or educational nature are not novels.

This is not a book for academics. I have written it in plain language so that any storyteller can understand it and begin applying these methods right away.

Throughout the book, I'll often use movies as examples. It's easier for you to watch a few two-hour movies to understand the examples than it is for you to read several books. It's also more likely that you've seen the movies I'll use than that you've read any particular book I might use as an example.

Take the time to actually watch the movies. Don't just take my word for it. It will pay off. The movies we'll use as examples are:

*Star Wars: A New Hope* (the original, a.k.a. "Episode 4". 1978)
*Iron Man 2* (2010)
*The Godfather* (1972)
*Hitch* (2005)
*Wonder Woman* (2017)
*Indiana Jones and the Raiders of the Lost Ark* (1981)
*It's a Wonderful Life* (1947)
*The Matrix* (1999)
*The Hunger Games* (2012)

Throughout this book, I'll use the pronouns *she* and *he* interchangeably and at random to refer to characters or a book reader. Obviously, your characters can be of either gender. My use of the pronouns shouldn't be construed to imply that a hero, for instance, can only be male. This saves us a lot of awkward "he or she" type language or the singular "they," which can be very confusing in this context.

I believe that if you apply these principles, you will write a great book. This method has helped so many people get out of the rut and actually finish projects. I can't wait to see what you produce once you're armed with this information.

You're no longer working alone. You have a team now. I'm going to be your coach and your guide, so that you can accomplish some of the incredible things you're imagining. Working together, we're going to change the world. I've done my part, and you're holding it in your hands. Now it's your turn to take this information, level up, and radically affect hearts and minds with your stories.

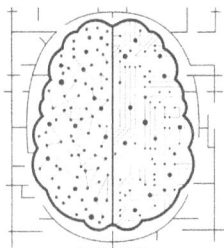

# INTRODUCTION

IN THE 4TH CENTURY BC, Aristotle noticed something peculiar. He observed that successful stories were told in three parts, with a well-defined beginning, middle, and end. He's sometimes credited with inventing modern story structure, but that's not quite true. Instead, he simply observed some common traits in all the good dramas he was watching. There were certain things that every good story did and all bad stories were missing.

This thing that he witnessed wasn't unique to ancient Greek society. It can be found in stories from around the world, throughout history, and in the modern era.

Do you realize that you've been hearing the same story over and over again? Superheroes, romances, even the world's oldest stories, are telling you the same tale.

It seems there's something instinctual about the way humans understand story. It's as if we're created with certain story markers embedded in us. Even if we can't explain it, there's something intuitive inside of us that can separate good story from bad story. While we each have our preferences for stories, these markers are nearly universal.

God gave me a gift to understand stories. I have an intuitive understanding of what makes stories "work." I don't know whether it came naturally to me, or it was the result of watching the same movies over and over as a kid. (We didn't have cable, and I just about memorized the fifty or so movies we had in the closet.) Either way, stories just make sense to me.

In my early twenties, I started to get involved in writers' groups and then God opened some doors for me to begin working with small publishers. He was providing a path for me to step into my calling—to do the thing He had made me to do. At the time, I had a natural instinct for stories and some handy experience with web marketing and coding. The e-book revolution was just kicking off, and I was well-suited to help publishers tackle the new opportunities and constraints of the digital book market. I did the digital stuff because it was a skill I could identify and trade, but it was story that I loved. Over time, my career grew to include more and more story, and less coding and marketing.

People started hiring me to critique their stories and to tell them how to fix them, and I started working as a developmental editor. I learned along the way that simply being able to say that a story worked or didn't work wasn't enough, even if I could also tell them how to make it better. I couldn't always expect my clients to just trust my intuition. The truth is that I worked with quite a few clients as a developmental editor before I really *knew* anything. Eventually, I had to figure out *why* stories worked.

And so I did. I began to put the pieces together and to look for commonalities in great stories. What kind of plot devices do great stories always include? What kinds of characters are always present? What kinds of characters are only sometimes present? I began to combine the commonalities and then restructure them again.

What I found was the Novel Matrix. I began to apply it to my clients' work, and not only did their work improve, but they also learned to become better writers in the process. Rather than just being a dictator who told them what to do, I became a partner with them, to really collaborate, and everyone grew in the process. When I could explain *why* their stories didn't work, rather than just telling them what was broken, it boosted them into a position to correct their technique and genuinely improve, rather than just patching the holes.

It's been long-established that humans have a psychological need for story. We have story-based memories. My dog knows impressions, but I seriously doubt that she has a narrative running through her head. She knows the leash in my hand is good, but I don't think she reminisces about that great walk we had in the park last October, when the leaves were in peak color and she crunched over the green husks of fallen walnuts.

Humans, however, know story. We think in story. We associate in story. It's how we understand the world. If you sit around a campfire for a while, someone will tell a story—a funny anecdote of something that happened recently or in their childhood. If you ride in the car for long enough with someone, eventually stories will fill the silence. You don't have to know the people in the story, you really don't have to care about the subject, the only commonality of experience is story itself.

And there are certain parameters that *work* in a story. There are factors that seem to permeate all successful stories with few exceptions. As writers, that's what we're interested in. What are the specific things that all good stories do?

What if you could learn to hit these invisible marks? What if you could guarantee that your story *worked*, but you could still color it with your perspective and no one would even know *how* you did it? They'd just know, somehow, that the story was satisfying and right.

Truthfully, I don't know which of the parameters I've discovered are unique to our time and place in 21st century America. I suspect that some of them are, but I know that many of them are not. Thanks to Aristotle, we know that much of what we'll discuss dates to at least the 4th century BC. We also see many of these markers present in ancient texts, both fiction and non-fiction. Even the Bible follows many of these conventions.

There's something mechanical about the way stories interface with our essential human psychology.

In Aristotle's day and in much of ours, the theory we'll discuss didn't exist. Sometimes writers stumbled upon it by accident and were successful, most of the time they didn't and weren't.

Joseph Campbell developed what he called the hero's journey in the 20th century with some similar ideas in a very long book called *The Hero with a Thousand Faces*. He was working off the backs of anthropologists and folklorists who had studied story in the blooming world of academia in the 19th century.

And it didn't stop there. Academics continue to debate and develop these theories today.

The problem is that, like much of academia, the theory is useless. It makes for good scholarly papers and intimidating conversations, but the academic world offers far more theory than application.

I don't mean that the study is useless. Knowledge is power and all that jazz. But it lacks practical application. It's more something to talk about than something to do.

Academics are under tremendous pressure to develop something new, to take the theory to its next step. But what happens when the truth is quite simple? The theories have become more elaborate than the subject itself, and the whole thing only circles back on itself in uselessness. The result is a convoluted mess of ideas about what constitutes a story.

The Novel Matrix boils all of that theory down to the essential elements and then it does something very unusual…it provides a practical application. I'm not going to try to impress you with some astounding new idea. I'm going to tell you what seems to be an old and simple thing—just one that's been buried.

There are certainly other helpful guides for writing a novel. However, the Novel Matrix strikes an important balance. Other guides I've seen are so vague as to leave the writer basically where they started (admittedly, after a lot of fun), or they're so specific that there really isn't much room left for the writer to craft his own story. It's practically a paint-by-number exercise.

By identifying and applying the essential elements we'll discuss, you'll be in a position to really dig in and get your wheels turning, but there's plenty of room for you to fill in the gaps, craft a story that's truly yours, and genuinely surprise your reader. This isn't just a technique for beginners, great books—books that go down in history—do the same things we're going to talk about.

This is not an academic treatise, so I won't make it any longer than it needs to be. I've done the hard work of distilling complex sources and filtering that through real-world experience.

I've used these exact tools to help hundreds of authors complete workable manuscripts, many of which have won awards and best-seller status.

Using the Novel Matrix method, you're going to write a story that "works." No first draft is perfect and every manuscript needs careful consideration and revision, but if you use this method you can be confident that audiences will be able to connect with your work and that it will satisfy their core need for story.

When you begin to understand story, something amazing happens. A novel project changes from a big, nebulous, fickle endeavor into a quantifiable project requiring a predictable amount of labor. When you can see the elements and how they interact with each other, you can approach the project methodically, completing one task at a time to a foreseeable outcome.

By applying these concepts, you'll be able to write a complete novel draft in less than 100 hours. You will certainly need to revise, but your draft will be complete and you'll be confident that you've crafted an excellent story.

Identifying the essential elements of the novel does not mean that your book will be formulaic or predictable. Quite the contrary. When you understand the rules, you're finally in a place to intentionally manipulate them!

Almost every great novel written in the last 100 years does what I'm about to show you, and you had no idea. These secrets were hidden just below the surface. There is no limit to what you can achieve with it. Greatness is no longer an elusive and fickle mistress, it's within your grasp.

If you're using this method well, your audience will be completely unaware that it's happening. They'll just know that it feels right, and they'll be open to what you have to tell them.

This is a structure and organizational manual, not a writing manual per se. There are so many great resources to learn more about showing and telling, writing compelling dialogue, and so many other elements of craft and technique. We won't cover them here. Along the way, I'll provide links to additional resources for writing craft, but our purpose in this text is solely to help you plan and execute a novel draft. I'm counting on you to develop your ability to write clear, beautiful prose and to marry that with the tools provided here.

God is the master storyteller. It should come as no surprise that many of the elements we'll discuss are also present in the biblical narrative. When you see the story that's built into our basic human psychology, and then you see how the biblical narrative follows the same pattern, you'll never doubt again where the story of this planet is going.

I want to change *your* world, so that you can change *the* world. The Novel Matrix will revolutionize the way that you understand story and approach your writing projects. I think you're going to be in a position to impact real audiences with your work.

Stories have tremendous power to affect hearts and minds. Armed with the tools of the Novel Matrix, you'll have a working vehicle to impact the world with the stories God has placed on your heart.

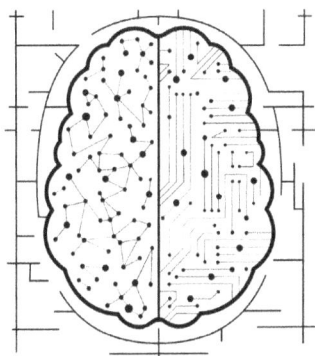

PART I

# UNDERSTANDING THE NOVEL MATRIX

# 1

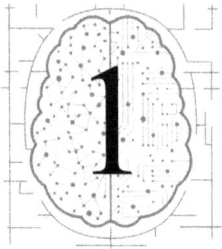

# STORY STRUCTURE

OUR STORIES ARE better today than the stories of old. There's a reason teenagers eat up *The Hunger Games* but have to be forced to read *A Tale of Two Cities*. The classics have a ton of value and we can learn so much from them, but the simple truth is that we have gotten better at telling stories over the past 100 years. This is not simply a question of taste, 19th century audiences would have liked *The Hunger Games* more too.

Our methods of storytelling are better aligned with human psychology than ever before. We've been learning. The novel is not an ancient art form. While we've seen examples of long-form narrative for a couple of thousand years—things like *The Iliad*—the printing press is less than 600 years old and literacy has only been commonplace for about 200 years. From the perspective of the history of the world, anything like commodified written stories are still brand new!

Consider a more obvious example. Film has only been around for about 100 years. While Charlie Chaplin has a certain nostalgic appeal, no one is arguing that his films compete creatively with Christopher

Nolan or Martin Scorsese of today. Every medium gets better over time. Books are no exception.

We've been learning and adapting as we go.

There are certain ways that you naturally understand stories. There are rules about *how the world works* that have to be followed or you won't really believe the story. Some ideas that you have about *how the world works* are unique to you and your life experience, but many of them seem to be hardwired in and shared by most humans.

Consider these two story premises:

- Story 1: Joe, a mild-mannered accountant and family man, wakes up on Wednesday morning and decides that he's going to murder every member of the Zambino crime family.

- Story 2: Joe, a mild-mannered accountant and family man, mistakenly gets involved with a client with shady dealings, and as a result of a case of mistaken identity, Joe's family is brutally murdered by the mafia. He wakes up on the Wednesday morning after the funerals with a plan to murder every member of the Zambino crime family.

The first story is ridiculous, but the second one seems reasonable, even if it's far-fetched. Maybe you even want to read it. (Don't worry, it's been written about a hundred times.)

Why is the second one reasonable? Because you intuitively understand that people don't make dramatic changes in their lives without a good reason. People don't just wake up one day and decide to be violent vigilantes.

You know people with serious problems who take no action to fix them, and they won't unless they're put in a position where they have to. That's the stuff of real life.

You know it's true about yourself even. If you're honest, you know that you have problems in your life right now that you could solve, but chances are you're not going to do a thing about them unless things get really bad.

I'm about fifteen pounds overweight right now and my car definitely needs new tires. I can tell you with confidence that I'm very unlikely to take action on either of these issues, even though I could fix either one.

So you have this simple rule that you intuitively know about stories. *People need a reason to take action.* If the characters in your stories make changes in their lives without a good reason, the reader won't really believe it.

Even readers who can't articulate that rule out loud still know it. If they read a story or watch a movie in which the rule is broken, they might come away saying something like, "I couldn't connect with the main character" or "I didn't buy the story." But what they're really saying is that the story violated what they know of *how the world works*.

In order to be effective storytellers, we need to identify the constructs that cause modern American readers to accept or reject stories. We need to know which constructs are absolute, which ones can be bent, and which ones can be broken. While we're at it, we need to be careful not to create any extra rules. We want to create a skeleton for the story, not a coffin.

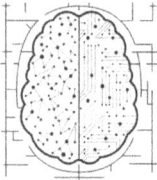

We want to create a skeleton for the story, not a coffin.

A novel is too big of a project to just wing it. A failed attempt could delay the launch of your writing career by months, if not years.

Would you bake a cake for the first time without a recipe? With company coming over?

Most of us wouldn't! Yet as writers, we seem to believe that we ought to just be able to whip up a novel, no big deal. If you ruin your cake, you've lost an hour and a few dollars in ingredients. If you ruin a novel, you've lost a hundred hours or more and maybe $1,000 in coffee. Why would we take a risk with such a big investment?

Cakes all have common elements. Flour, water, sugar, eggs. You can change the proportions of these ingredients for different types of cakes, and maybe throw in a few spices, but these are the essential elements of every cake.

According to Donald Miller, one of my favorite living authors, the recipe for stories is pretty simple, too: "A story is a character who wants something and overcomes conflict to get it."

Stories are setting, character, conflict, and plot. These are the essential elements of a story. With these four things, you always have a story. If one of these elements is missing, it's really not a story anymore. It may be a beautiful poem or vignette, but it's not a story.

By changing the proportion of these elements, you can change the nature of the story. Add a lot of character and a little conflict and you're baking literary fiction. Get creative and double your portion of setting and now it's science fiction.

With the Novel Matrix, you can write a book in 100 hours, and you will know from day one that it will work. New authors working without any help typically spend hundreds or even thousands of hours on a manuscript before they're willing to call it "finished," and even then it might not *work*.

The process of writing a successful novel all boils down to an intentional balance of those critical four ingredients: setting, character, conflict, and plot.

## TOO FAT OR TOO SKINNY?

Beginning novelists often struggle to capture the right amount of information on the page. Some novels are jam-packed with too many ideas to keep track of, while others seem to be stretching and stretching a simple idea and there just isn't enough content to go around.

I refer to this as novels that are too fat or too skinny.

Novels that are *too skinny* really don't have enough material. Maybe there's a cool character, setting, or plot twist, but it's like all the ideas have been stretched as far as they'll possibly go to get to a novel-length work. The idea could maybe support a 20,000 word story, but the author has stretched it into 70,000 words.

Novels that are *too fat* have way too much material. It feels as if the author is cramming every idea they ever thought of together. They made a fruit cake, which everyone knows is disgusting. The reader is forced to follow multiple competing plot lines, twenty important characters, and commentary on ten different social issues. This could be five books, but it's all smashed into one.

The Novel Matrix, in the hands of a discerning writer, puts the right amount of information on the page. Before you even begin writing, you'll know if you have enough content in your mind to fill a complete novel or if you need to continue brainstorming. You'll also know if you're overloading it and need to save some of the content for book two.

Memoirs and creative nonfiction also require the sensibilities of the Novel Matrix.

Successful memoirists take the events of real life, but then pick and choose and rearrange those events to fit the story constructs that we'll discuss. Bill Bryson doesn't just always happen to live perfect stories. Instead, he takes the real events of his life and rearranges them, using many of the principles here, so that readers can connect deeply with the content.

Memoirs often struggle to stay on a consistent track and present complexity in the right places. The Novel Matrix method will keep you on target.

## ARE YOU A PLOTTER OR A PANTSER?

There's a bizarre thing that happens in the process of writing in which characters *become themselves*. In some way I don't fully understand, the author dissociates from their creation, and your own characters begin to surprise you! This is a beautiful part of the creative process and yields better results. The characters become more realistic, more empathetic, and entirely more interesting. But this can't happen if your book is over-planned. We need at least a little bit of room for our characters to breathe and be spontaneous.

*A plotter or a pantser*...this question makes its rounds among writers.

Plotters meticulously plan every element of their novel before they begin. All of the plot points and characters are articulated, writing is just putting flesh on the bones of an outline.

Pantsers write by the seat of their pants. Theoretically, they just show up with an idea (or not), and start writing to see where it goes.

Most new authors have a natural bent, some way that makes sense to them to approach a big writing project.

The problem is that plotting is too strict for many creatives, yet pantsing often fails to yield workable results.

If you just make up the story as you go along (pantsing), it's so easy to spend hours and hours on a manuscript only to get to a point where you realize that your idea doesn't work at all. After investing so much, you may spend another hundred hours rewriting or end up scrapping the project all together. With a little planning and forethought, you could have predicted the problem before you got so far and before you wasted so much time.

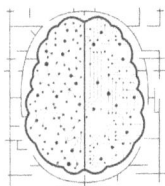

LET ME ADDRESS a common objection. There are a few notable examples of hyper-successful self-proclaimed pantsers like Stephen King and Agatha Christie. Ironically, in the final product, these authors are doing what we'll describe in the Novel Matrix. In fact, we could use many of their books as examples. We don't know whether they were born with this knowledge, received it by divine revelation, or simply learned it intuitively by trial and error through many repetitions. However, Stephen King wrote at least five novels prior to *Carrie*, which was arguably his first book that "worked," and he also has a genius IQ.

Taking the time to learn a method could save you a million words that it would take you to "discover" your own way. Most likely, you'll write a million words only to find that you end up at the Novel Matrix anyway.

A novel project is too big of an undertaking to wing it.

But, we don't want the plan to be too rigid (plotting). That can take the fun right out of it! Years ago, a popular romance publisher offered a course in which they would train you page by page how to write a bodice ripper novel. The publisher knew what would sell, and so they turned it into a paint-by-number exercise. If you followed their pattern, you could basically fill in the names, setting, and a few creative details and have a "good" book. Or at least a book that would sell at the grocery store.

Anybody could do it. But then what's the fun? Where's the artistry? Where's the self-expression?

The solution is *plantsing*. Plantsing dictates that we know the core elements of our story before we begin. We put all the major elements in a well-constructed plan so that we know the story is viable. However, there's enough margin in the framework for the author to be spontaneous. There's enough space to allow the characters to bloom and do things that surprise you.

Plantsing is to get in the car and say, "We're going to grandma's today," but to have only generally determined your route and with your eye out for an interesting place to stop for lunch on the way.

## THE VALLEY OF THE SHADOW OF DEATH

According to a popular survey, about 265 million Americans would like to write a book. Most of them will never even start, but even among those that do, most will never finish. In my experience, about 1% of people who "want to write a book" will ever actually complete one.

Whether you plot or pants, for most authors, the results are about the same. Most new authors get about 20–30% of the way through the first draft and then just stop. I call this the "valley of the shadow of death".

At this critical mark, almost everybody starts to get a little bored with their own project. You've invested enough time that it's stopped being so much fun and it's started to feel a bit like work. It's probably been at least a couple of weeks, and your friends aren't nearly as excited to hear about it. It's so easy to take a week off from writing, only to forget about it all together, or to chase a shiny new idea that popped into your mind.

For natural pantsers (writing the story as it comes), confidence is a game changer when you're plodding through the valley of the shadow of death. Without a plan, it's so easy for the pantser to say, "This story is stupid and wasn't going to work anyway," or "I've written myself into a corner," and they're very likely correct.

However, if you have a loose plan and you already know you're working on a story that is very likely to come together, it becomes much easier to buckle down, exercise a little discipline, and push yourself through those hard parts.

For natural plotters, a little flexibility in the plan keeps it fun and exciting. Forcing yourself not to over-plot the book, and to allow those characters to come alive and surprise you, will keep the project new and interesting.

In either case, plantsing is the solution. The Novel Matrix provides enough structure to achieve that middle ground—viable yet with still enough room for creativity.

The Novel Matrix is designed to give you structure without overwhelming your creativity with rigidity.

## FEAR OF FORMULA

Did you know that many high-end wedding cake bakers use a boxed cake mix for the base of their cake?

Why? Because the base is not where the artistry is. That's not where the artist wants to take a risk.

The artist just needs a cake that will work, a structure that will taste pretty good and not collapse. The risk, the artistry, is in the decoration, in the details.

Wedding cakes are absolutely works of art. But the artist can only show off their amazing work because it's built on something stable. There's something solid underneath that they can count on to work.

When you write a book, you need a story structure that works. Then you have the opportunity to layer your artistry on top of it. There is a difference between structure and formula.

Are *Iron Man 2* and *The Godfather* the same story? How about *Hitch* and *Star Wars*? Of course not! Yet they all follow the Novel Matrix structure.

What about virtually every bestselling novel of the last fifty years? Are some of them "formulaic?" Sure. But that has far more to do with the author's lack of artistry than with using a structure.

We could extend the analogy to all kinds of art forms. Hot rods, for instance, are an art form too. If you go to a car show, you'll see some amazing cars. Each one is a unique expression of the creator's values. Some are made to look like pure muscle, others have an antique vibe. "Rat rods" are a genre of hot rod that are intentionally made to look junky on the outside but are super high-end in the mechanics.

Despite all of the expression, artistry, and unique outcomes, every single one of those cars will have some similar components. Every car at the show will have a motor, transmission, axles, tires, steering wheel…and the list goes on. Does that mean they're not art? Because they share common components? Of course not! In fact, that's what makes them hot rods.

If I made a "hot rod" and didn't include a motor or tires because I'm "creative," anybody into hot rods would rightly say, "That's a cool sculpture or something, but it's not a hot rod."

Your novel is the same. The structural elements that we'll be discussing are what make it a novel. Setting, character, conflict, and plot are the things that define your work as a novel. You need to understand these things and understand what your reader expects. There's nothing formulaic about it.

Most certainly, there are exceptions to what I'll be describing here—successful stories that don't follow the structure. We live in a media rich society, and every once in a while a story will burst forth that breaks the mold. However, the Novel Matrix is the most common structure you'll see in literature, especially in modern American sto-

BRAD PAUQUETTE

rytelling. Most stories that deviate from these essential elements are radically unsuccessful. Master this stuff first, then you can break the rules on purpose to achieve a specific effect.

There are also many other editors who have proposed and written books on story structure, but who have taken it to the level of formula, down to listing all of the specific scenes that your book needs to include and in what order. That is formulaic. It's like buying a hot rod kit, where you put together someone else's work and just pick the paint colors.

The Novel Matrix will help you understand the basic structure of the novel—the most essential elements of the recipe—while still giving you all the freedom to express your unique artistry and produce a story that is anything but formulaic.

You're going to write a great book. The structure that the Novel Matrix provides is going to ensure that your story works, so that your creativity, your message, and your wonderful prose shine brightly.

Structure isn't a limitation. Instead, it's an opportunity for creativity and expression. Structure is your springboard so that your ideas can take flight.

# 2

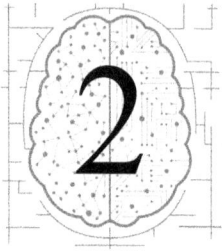

# THE NOVEL MATRIX

IF WE'RE GOING to write amazing stories, we need a vehicle that works. This is how we change the world.

We'll begin by understanding stories, then in Part II we'll apply these concepts to a brand new idea.

The basic constructs of the Novel Matrix are: one universe, three acts, five conflicts, and seven characters.

These elements interact with each other. We'll address them briefly here and then take them in depth one-at-a-time in the following chapters.

## A SETTING ("THE UNIVERSE")

Every story needs to take place in a well-defined universe. The reader brings certain rules to the story for *how the world works*, other rules are created by the author. Most of what the reader brings has to do with human nature, and you have the opportunity to define the rest.

You know people that live in a different universe than you do. You're willing to accept that not everyone's rules are the same. Things work differently in the corporate boardroom than they do in the

Walmart break room. But in both situations, people are people. The social and even physical rules can be different, but people are people.

In order to accept a story as a reader, you have to first understand what the rules of the universe are. Readers will accept a story about laser guns, magic, or hunky men that come to the rescue if the author establishes those rules. Without a defined universe, those things are all absurd.

## A PLOT

Change doesn't happen overnight. You know that most people aren't successful at anything on their first try. It takes time to be successful. Anything worth doing means dealing with dead ends, disappointments, surprises, and betrayals. As humans, we have to learn our lessons the hard way, and hopefully we can apply those lessons to reach our goals.

The events of a story unfold over time. The main character (a.k.a. the "protagonist" or "hero") will go on a journey with three distinct parts. The protagonist will lose everything dear to him and be forced into action, he will try to overcome his obstacles but fail, and ultimately he will learn a lesson and be successful.

## CONFLICT

As consumers of stories, we tend to focus on the one big conflict that gets resolved in any story. If you were asked about the plot of *Star Wars*, you might say, "Luke Skywalker destroys the Death Star." For *Indiana Jones*, you might say, "Indiana Jones steals the Ark of the Covenant from the Nazis."

But that's not *how the world works*. Things aren't really that simple. And the movie wasn't that simple either. Your brain took a bunch of different things that were competing for attention in the movie, and rendered out the most important one. But there was more there.

In your real life, right now you have a vast array of potential problems. Your world is seemingly infinitely complex. You have relationships with dozens of people, maybe more. You might be actively addressing a couple of things you want to change in your life, and there are more things that you know could be better that pester you in big and little ways—that issue at work you're trying to ignore, that thing you're wondering if you should talk to a doctor about, the warning light on the dashboard of the car.

A great novel needs enough conflict to simulate the intricacies of real life, but needs to be simple enough that the reader can understand the story. With exactly five well-articulated conflicts, an author can represent the complexity of real life and *how the world works* without making the story too complex or too long.

## CHARACTERS

Of course a great story needs a protagonist, which is almost always the main character. But everybody needs a little help from their friends. That's *how the world works*. Most successful stories also include a sidekick, a guide, a frenemy, and a victim. And every story, even a character-driven story, needs bad guys—usually two of them.

## INTO THE MIXING POT

These elements—the universe, plot, conflicts, and characters—are articulated in the planning stages of a novel, and then thrown together in scenes. Something special comes out.

When we read and watch great stories, as students of story, we need to start asking, "How?" *How did the storyteller make me feel that way? How did the storyteller keep me awake that night?*

I studied creative writing in college, and I took several literature classes. Once I even spent an entire semester on Jane Austen's *Mansfield Park*. The exposure to sources I wouldn't have ordinarily read was helpful, but I gained very little useful information for my writing from these classes. We were using the wrong language. Most of our discussion of any text was based on identifying themes and irony.

Themes and irony are, of course, essential to great literature. But that's just the "what." The question we should have been asking is "how?" *How did Jane Austen make you feel that way? What did Flannery O'Connor do to embed irony in the story?*

The answers are in the Novel Matrix. Themes and irony exist at the confluence of character, conflicts, setting, and plot. These things combine together in predictable ways, but sometimes yield unexpected results.

When college literature classes discuss themes and irony, they're really trying to have a conversation about the relationship between character, setting, conflicts, and plot. They're just doing it in an esoteric way. (*Academia*, am I right?)

What would happen if we started teaching high schoolers about the mechanics of story? What if we focused as much on *why* and *how* readers interact with the stories they love? I suspect that such an approach would fascinate many students who previously couldn't connect with their assigned reading.

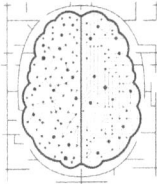

---

THROUGH THE COURSE of the book we'll discuss many popular stories. I primarily chose my favorites of the most popular movies of the past fifty years as examples because many people have seen them and they're easy to find if you haven't. I strongly encourage you to take the time to watch these movies and test the theory. Don't take my word for it. I primarily use movies because it's much easier and quicker to watch a movie and observe the Novel Matrix in action than it is to read a whole book.

Many movies are based on books, as you know, and the stories are usually simplified. There just isn't space in a two-hour film to accomplish everything the book did. Keep in mind that the reverse is true as well. Your book will need to be slightly more complex than the movies you're used to watching.

Nonetheless, films are long-form stories, and the same elements are present. For our purposes of understanding how stories work, we can observe these elements just as well in movies as we can in novels.

---

A book is a relationship between a writer and a reader. The writer only brings half of the material to the table. That material gets filtered through the reader's life experience, expectations, and philosophy to yield something special. There's an effect on our hearts. In my opinion, that's way more fun and helpful to explore.

While an author may start with relatively simple ingredients—universe, plot, conflict, and character—when these ingredients combine together they often birth unintended nuances and complexity, like so many chemicals bubbling over a beaker.

After a cake has been baked, can you discern the individual flavors of the original ingredients that were mixed together? Usually not! All of those individual ingredients that went in become a unified whole in the process of creation. A story is the same.

As we learn more about the ingredients of story, I'll be using my interpretation of the movies we're discussing. As any good college literature class proves, we could spend an hour discussing the nuanced primary conflict of a story. I say the novel's about *heritage*, you say it's about *family*. An hour goes by and we've played a rousing game of *What Do Words Mean?* A semester goes by and we've each written a six-page paper. What will we have gained?

In fact, even if I see a movie with friends and we sit around and chat about it, we likely wouldn't come to a consensus. Your understanding of a story is unique to you, because your relationship with the storyteller is unique. The way you understand the world, the similarities and differences to your own experiences, and your aspirations all affect the way you digest the story.

With the examples we'll use to explore the Novel Matrix, you may have slightly different conclusions about some elements of the story. That's okay. Don't get hung up on it.

The irony of the Novel Matrix is that as an author you will carefully plan your novel, and in fifty years some college literature class will find whatever they want in it. They'll discuss themes and elements you did not intend, but to those readers, they'll be real.

The important thing is that you understand how the Novel Matrix elements relate to one another, and that you carefully plan them when you develop your novel. Ultimately, your readers will find all kinds of cool nuanced things that you were so smart and insightful to write!

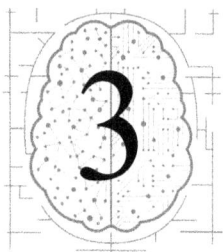

# ONE UNIVERSE

IN STORY, THERE'S NO SUCH THING as the "real world." It's the storyteller's responsibility to teach the reader what is possible and what is normal.

Every story happens in a fictional universe, even if it's a seemingly true story or you perceive it to be happening in the "real world." The real world does not exist between the pages of a book. Everything must be defined.

A "universe" of a story includes the social, physical, spiritual, and emotional parameters and expectations for the setting of the story. A story must answer these questions:

- Where are we?

- What's normal here?

- What is exceptional?

- What is impossible?

Ironically, a story must establish the rules of the universe so that later those rules can be broken.

Surprise is one of your greatest tools as a storyteller. We feel surprised when something violates our expectations. That means that in order to be surprised, a reader must have an expectation. If the author doesn't teach me what's supposed to be impossible, how will I be surprised when the protagonist breaks barriers to do it?

Consider this example: Bruce Lee, a kung fu master, knocks every bad guy out with a single punch or kick…until he meets the big, bad boss. When he punches the big guy, the brute just laughs and barely moves. Now we're surprised.

We only know that this guy is really bad news because for the past twenty minutes the story established that a normal guy goes down in one Bruce Lee punch. The rule is, "Regular guys go down in one punch." The really bad guy violates the rule. That's how we know he's special.

When Trinity jumps a hundred feet between rooftops in *The Matrix* for the first time, it's surprising. Why? Because until that moment, Trinity seemed to be subject to our regular understanding of gravity. She'd done some cool kung fu stuff, but otherwise, the storytellers confirmed gravity as I know it in my own life. All of the policemen in the scene also conformed to seemingly normal gravity and were as surprised as I was when Trinity broke the rules.

The rules of the universe aren't just about physics. A good story also defines social and cultural norms.

In the BBC series *Downton Abbey*, the story establishes a social norm that servants do not speak freely to the members of the aristocratic family. This is a rule of the story's universe.

As viewers, we learn the rule by witnessing it in action. We see how the servants avert their attention from the aristocrats. When a character violates the rule, we see that character chastised by the butler. When someone breaks the rule, we're surprised and we pay attention to what happens next. "Why did they do that? It must be important."

In romance stories, usually a character will violate a well-established social rule. For instance, Capulets do not associate with Montagues (*Romeo and Juliet)*, or daughters of white collar fathers do not have serious relationships with blue collar boys (*The Notebook*).

Because we have learned the rules, the story becomes notable. If no one teaches you that Sharks don't hang out with Jets (*West Side Story*) then the story doesn't make any sense!

## COMMON ELEMENTS OF THE UNIVERSE

There are a few rules that every story needs to establish. The genre will dictate which rules are most important. Here are some rule sets that need to be defined for virtually any story:

## SOCIAL NORMS

How do normal people act around each other? What rules govern their relationships? Consider how different the rules are in the TV show *Friends* compared to *The Three Musketeers*.

In one story it's routine for the characters to be super rude and sarcastic to even their closest friends. In the other story, an offhanded remark might land a character in a fatal duel.

What should surprise the audience? In *Friends*, if a character makes even a halfway kindhearted and decent remark, the audience will *awwww* because they're surprised. On the other hand, in *The Three Musketeers*, we would gasp in anticipation of the forthcoming thrashing for an accidental insult.

For many stories, the author must define typical attitudes regarding marriage, sexual relations, drug and alcohol use, religion, and petty crime, among others.

## MAGIC AND SUPERNATURAL

Does magic or supernatural activity exist in the story? Do normal people believe in it or have access to it? What is the prevailing explanation for unexplainable events?

Consider *Harry Potter,* in which magic is routine, versus *Freaky*

*Friday,* in which a magical occurrence will be a defining moment of a character's life.

For stories with a Christian worldview, is it normal for people to be healed by prayer or is that an exceptional event? Do angels interact with humans regularly or infrequently? Is it normal for people to hear from God or is that the mark of a special gift? Are clergy members usually good or usually suspicious? What role do demons play in addiction and personality disorders? The story must define it.

## PHYSICAL ACTIONS/REACTIONS

A story must establish what happens when somebody gets punched, falls from somewhere high, or gets shot at.

In *Back to the Future,* Biff is knocked out cold with a single punch. In *Shanghai Noon*, Owen Wilson and Jackie Chan are beaten up for two hours straight with virtually no ill effects.

Remember that the rules allow a reader to be surprised when a character is able to violate or overcome them.

## ROMANCE AND LOVE

Does true love exist or is romance a matter of finding someone with a compatible personality?

The overriding theme of *The Notebook* is that Noah and Allie are meant to be together. Neither character can ever be as in love with anyone else, because their fates are intertwined.

In *The Godfather*, Michael loves Kay, but when he has to leave the country, he moves on, then loves and marries Apollonia. When she dies, he returns to America and loves Kay again.

What's the value of a kiss? In some stories, "the kiss" is tantamount to marriage. It's the realization of destiny. In other stories, a kiss is just a kiss.

If the audience doesn't know ahead of time that a kiss is actually *the* kiss, they'll lose the magic.

## SERENDIPITY

Every story has things that just work out. Why is that? Is that due to God, fate, superstitious luck, or coincidence?

In *The Matrix*, Neo is chosen for a reason. He has a destiny to fulfill. Contrast that to *Apollo 13*, in which the characters do their best with their big brains to figure out a solution, and then they get lucky.

## TECHNOLOGY

What technology is available in the story's universe? As importantly, who has access to the technology? In *Star Wars*, laser guns and space travel are commonplace. Most people seem to have access to such things. In *The Hunger Games*, things like hover ships exist, but almost no one has access to them.

What exists in your universe? What do normal people have access to?

## BOREDOM = CONFUSION

A lot of fantasy is absolutely perplexing if you don't know the difference between an ogre and a troll before you start. Sci-fi is confusing if you don't know what FTL means. Confusion prevents a reader from connecting with a story, and often leads to feelings of "boredom."

Readers often have trouble stepping into new genres not because they wouldn't like them but because they don't understand them. Most readers love all genres when they're introduced to them in a way that helps them to understand the rules of the universe.

Tom Clancy is a great example. Some people find his books mind-numbingly tedious, others find them absolutely riveting. This has far more to do with the reader's ability to understand the intricacies of the story than it is a matter of taste. That's not an insult to readers that don't like Tom Clancy, the fact is that he uses a tremendous amount of military and political vocabulary. For instance, you need to know that a young lieutenant outranks an experienced sergeant and that there are protocols and expectations in place because of that. Clancy often relies on the reader already knowing the rules of a conventional American military universe, rather than educating the reader.

If a reader doesn't know the language, he's going to miss a lot of the depth and complexity of Clancy's stories, and find them "boring."

The Marvel Universe suffers the same fate. Part of what makes the stories interesting for Marvel fans are the ways in which the stories connect together—the tiny hints that superfans see where the stories overlap. If a viewer steps into a Marvel movie for the first time and doesn't know the universe, the movie will only be half as interesting as it is for a superfan.

The next time a friend says something is "boring" that you find riveting, ask yourself if you can help them understand the universe, so that they appreciate the depth and complexity of the stories like you do.

As writers, we need to be a good friend to our reader and help her to step confidently into our story's universe.

Oftentimes, breakout genre fiction is effective because it does a great job of welcoming new readers into the genre. *Twilight* broke out at least in part because you didn't have to be a vampire superfan to understand the story. Stephenie Meyer welcomed readers to learn vicariously through Bella.

Suzanne Collins made a careful and easy on-ramp for new readers to step into the post-apocalyptic world of *The Hunger Games*. Young female readers who would typically reject sci-fi fell in love with the book because Collins gave them an opportunity to learn and engage with the conventions of the genre.

## ONBOARDING A READER

"Jargon" is a set of words that only make sense to a particular group of people or in a particular setting. You probably use jargon in your workplace and even in your own home.

I tell my kids "teeth and potty," which in itself is a ridiculous and meaningless phrase. My kids know it means to brush their teeth, put on pajamas, use the bathroom, and get in bed.

If you've ever worked in a restaurant, you've probably heard someone say "eighty-six," as in "eighty-six the New York strip special." To someone who doesn't live in that world, that's a nonsense phrase, but in restaurant jargon it means that you've run out of something and to stop selling it.

We learn jargon all the time, mostly by context. Virtually any time you enter a new environment, like a workplace, club, church, or an online community, you're exposed to words and phrases you've never used before.

Special care has to be taken to help a reader into the universe. Stories don't usually give the reader a written list of rules and vocabulary. Instead, just like the jargon you learn in everyday life, great stories give the reader opportunities to learn the universe through exposure and context.

*Dune* by Frank Herbert is a tremendous example of this. Modern editions of the book often include a glossary of terms in the back, but the original printings did not. Herbert simply dropped the reader into a complex universe with no explanations. We "see" the rules in action, and readers, by and large, are able to pick it up and understand the story.

To return to *Downton Abbey*, no one ever has to explain that servants don't socialize with the aristocracy. Instead, we simply observe the rule in action over and over again. We see the characters respecting the social rule, and we also see characters chastised or punished for breaking the rule. Readers are smart—if they're given an opportunity to observe something, they'll put the pieces together.

Many stories successfully use the "stupid guy/smart guy" technique when the story requires more elaborate explanations. A stupid, young, or naive character follows around a smart or experienced character asking "What's that?" "What does this mean?" and "How does this work?" The smart guy answers all of those questions in dialogue, and it's often a great opportunity for humor and character development.

As readers, we relate to the stupid guy. We needed those answers too. By living vicariously through a cute or fun character, we get the answers we need without feeling patronized.

In the opening scene of the 2004 *Battlestar Galactica* TV series, the camera briefly follows a public relations guy as he gives a tour of the spaceship, explaining the technology as he goes. It feels organic to the scene, but those explanations are for our benefit.

In the first episode of *Friday Night Lights* (2006), a TV news reporter follows the football team around and asks a lot of questions. The reporter, as a character, is able to introduce tons of information, expectations, and "rules" very quickly.

In the first act of *Knives Out*, detective Benoit Blanc (Daniel Craig) interviews the other characters to fill in loads of backstory and information about the universe of the story.

Pay attention to how stories build the universe. There are infinite creative ways to *show* the rules of the universe. Keep your eyes peeled for original ways storytellers employ the "stupid guy/ smart guy" routine.

## UNIVERSE = GENRE

In many ways, the universe defines the genre.

Mario Puzo modeled his book *The Godfather* off of a classic Zane Grey western novel, *The Heritage of the Desert*. In Grey's tale, ranching families have a longstanding rivalry which leads to the deaths and vengeance killings of many members of the family. Puzo took the concept and adapted it to New York crime families. He simply changed the universe, and updated the location, technology, and social rules, and suddenly it was a new story in a new genre.

As long as you're not copying specific language and you're truly making the story your own, it is fair game to borrow story mechanics in creative writing. Take a story you love, then change the universe and change the emphasis. You'll have a new story in a new genre.

The same exact story, placed in a new universe, will yield a completely different genre.

The universe is powerful, and it's often overlooked. There is no such thing as "just normal."

## CONFIRM IT:

Most writers know about the importance of establishing a setting within a scene, but we overlook the universe as a storytelling tool.

When you're armed with universe as a tool of the story, you're in a powerful position to develop themes right under the reader's nose.

Watch a movie or consider a novel you've recently read. What are the rules of the universe? Using the provided worksheet, take the time to map them out.

To help this idea take root, ponder the universe and how the "rules" developed your understanding of the story and its themes.

Consider the following questions:

- How did the author or filmmaker establish the rules of the universe?

- Did the creator explain the rules or *show* the rules in effect? How?

- Did the creator provide a character through whom you could learn the rules?

- At any time, did the story utilize the "stupid guy/ smart guy" routine?

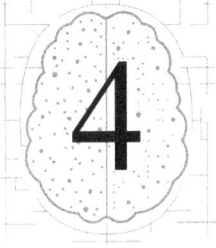

# 4

# THREE ACTS

ANY NOVEL-LENGTH WORK stated in one sentence sounds ridiculous.

- Farm boy destroys the biggest, baddest superweapon in the history of the universe. (*Star Wars*)

- University professor stops Nazis from using the biblical Ark of the Covenant to take over the world. (*Indiana Jones and the Raiders of the Lost Ark*)

- Jaded romance consultant finds true love with a reporter determined to expose and destroy him. (*Hitch*)

- Roman general is sold as a slave, becomes a famous gladiator, and assassinates the emperor. (*Gladiator*)

For any of these stories, it is completely ridiculous to think that the protagonist from the beginning of the story could accomplish the big thing at the end of the book. But the character undergoes a transformative journey that makes the impossible possible.

In a great novel, the author makes something ridiculous seem plausible.

A series of events will transform the protagonist into a new person who is now capable of doing a thing that was previously impossible for him. In American storytelling today and throughout history, the most common method used to accomplish this transformation (by far) and the most easily understood and relatable to readers (by a lot) is the three-act structure.

Aristotle is first credited with discovering the three-act structure over two thousand years ago. He saw that great stories have a developed beginning, middle, and end. Today, the three-act structure is a tool to take the reader on a journey that transforms the ridiculous into the plausible.

The three-act structure shares a close relationship with the psychology of story. It's almost as if it evolved organically.

Aristotle didn't invent the structure, he was just describing something natural that he saw working. In his time, it didn't seem to be something anyone knew they were doing. It was something that good storytellers just seemed to stumble upon.

Here's how the three acts break down. You'll immediately recognize this as the stuff of most long-form media you consume.

**Act 1:** The protagonist, or main character, is presented with an impossible task. At first, he refuses the task, but then he loses something that's important to him. When the protagonist hits "rock bottom," he's forced into action.

**Act 2:** The protagonist tries to accomplish the impossible task, but does it incorrectly. Sometimes he tries to solve the problem in the wrong way, other times he does the right thing incompetently. Now the bad guys are really upset, and things get worse than ever before.

**Act 3:** Just when things couldn't get any worse, the protagonist learns a lesson which enables him to perform the impossible task. Usually with the help of his new friends, he rises to the challenge and wins the day.

Throughout this book, I'll frequently use the word "hero" interchangeably with "protagonist" to describe the main character. Don't let that fool you. The sequence described here applies equally to every genre. You'll find it in literary fiction, romance, and all manner of modern fiction. Even if your genre doesn't have main characters that you'd typically consider "heroic," they're still the hero for our purposes.

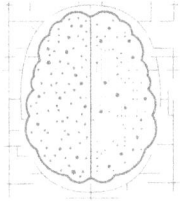

WHILE SOME OF the plot points we'll discuss are similar to other methods, the structure I'll describe is different from other novel-planning methods. Fair warning: don't try to combine this with another method, it won't work. You'll end up more confused than ever before. Pick one method that works for you and fully commit yourself to it.

## RISING AND FALLING ACTION

The concept of *rising and falling action* relates to the protagonist's changing success and failure through the story.

When the protagonist's life gets worse and he gets further from accomplishing his goal, this is "falling" action.

When the protagonist's life gets better and he gets closer to accomplishing his goal, this is "rising" action.

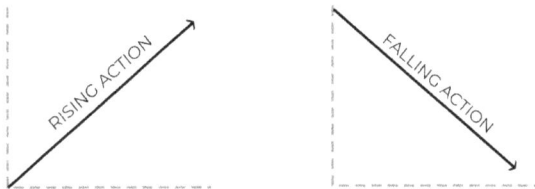

### A FEW EXAMPLES

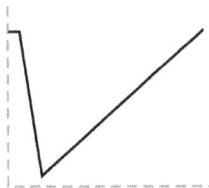

A RICH MAN *SUDDENLY* LOSES HIS MONEY, THEN SLOWLY EARNS IT BACK

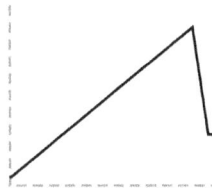

A POOR MAN SLOWLY BECOMES WEALTHY, BUT SUDDENLY LOSES *MOST* OF IT

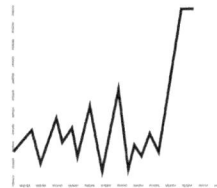

A MAN STRUGGLES WITH MONEY ALL HIS LIFE, THEN PUBLISHES A BESTSELLING BOOK
*RESULTS NOT TYPICAL*

If a character's goal is to get rich, and he starts out poor and gets a lot of money through the story, the story arc has *risen*. According to the character's goal, he started out poor and got rich. He rose.

If instead, he starts out rich and gets poor, then the story arc has *fallen*.

When we talk about rising and falling action, we're generally talking about long timelines. What's the overall trajectory of the character over thousands of words? However, that does not mean that everything that happens must be good in a rising action section, or that everything must be bad in a falling action section. Rising and falling action both carry the tension of minor victories and setbacks.

NOBODY EXPLAINS IT BETTER THAN KURT VONNEGUT

CHECK IT OUT ON YOUTUBE:
"KURT VONNEGUT,
SHAPE OF STORIES"

When we're talking about the shape of stories and rising and falling action, the most important points of the story are the sharp turns—the *vertices*. What happens in a story that causes the protagonist's arc to dramatically change direction?

## THE THREE-ACT STRUCTURE

In the following section, I'll use *Star Wars* as our example. *Star Wars* is undeniably one of the most important stories of the past fifty years and has shaped our culture in so many ways. Yet when you examine it, it's a relatively simplistic story. All of the elements we're discussing are in plain sight. All of the bad guys and good guys are easy to identify and it's easy to see when things are tending to get better and when things are tending to get worse.

Take the time to watch *Star Wars*. In the appendixes of this book, you'll find additional complete examples.

When we use films to study story, something becomes obvious that is harder to see in books: the amount of time between important events is critical.

Book readers, just like film watchers, experience a book as a function of time. A reader is internally aware of the passage of real time as she experiences the events of a book.

Film makers know that you have about forty minutes to beat up your protagonist before he needs to take action. That will buy you another forty minutes to get to the lesson the protagonist needs to learn. Then you have another forty minutes to wrap it all up and make everyone happy.

A 50,000-80,000 word novel is a four to eight hour time investment for the reader. That's of course longer than a two hour movie, but the principle still holds true. The reader will permit the novel a certain amount of time to get to the next important thing before she begins to feel bored or frustrated with the story.

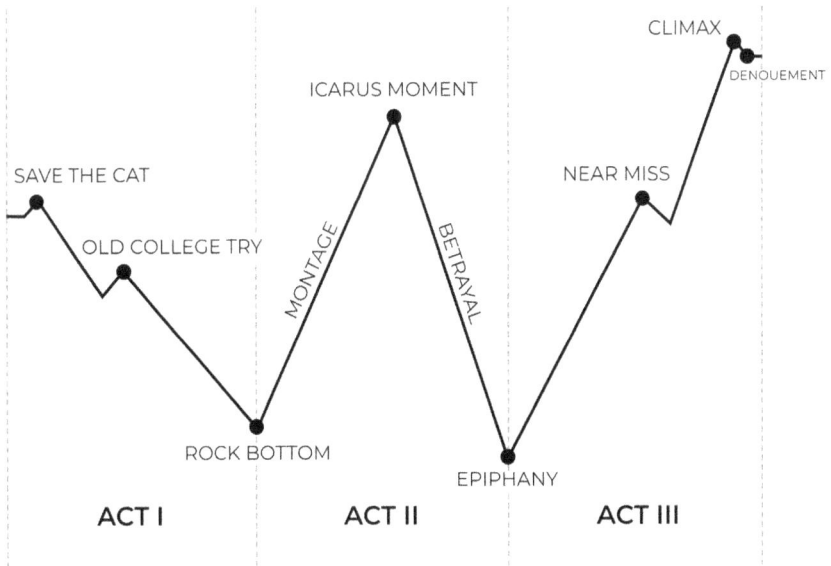

CLIMAX

DENOUEMENT

ICARUS MOMENT

SAVE THE CAT

NEAR MISS

OLD COLLEGE TRY

MONTAGE

BETRAYAL

ROCK BOTTOM

EPIPHANY

ACT I            ACT II            ACT III

The three-act structure keeps the velocity of critical events moving swiftly enough to maintain the attention of a reader. When the story changes between rising and falling action, it resets the reader's attention span. The story can't wander around for hours. The reader needs specific events to relate to. These events create a hard pin in the reader's understanding of the story, as if you're buying more time to tell your story.

When we lose those obvious turning points in the story, the story is "flat" and we're much more likely to lose the attention of the reader because she won't feel like the story is progressing.

Those hard turns (vertices) are the places where the story transitions between rising and falling action.

If we explain the plot of a book or movie to a friend, we focus on those hard turns in the story and skip the in-between parts. We focus on the events in which the protagonist's fortune suddenly changes. Those hard turns stick in our memory. If the story doesn't make hard turns, the story won't be memorable.

Remember that the purpose of the three-act structure is for the protagonist to accomplish an Impossible Thing. The character at the beginning of the story couldn't possibly accomplish what they'll do at the end. Over the course of the story, the protagonist will collect skills, values, relationships, and resources that make the Impossible Thing possible.

While we'll initially look at an action-adventure example because the pieces are so obvious to see, the same principles of story structure apply to *every genre*—romance, literary fiction, family saga, memoir.

Let's examine the three-act structure in more detail, with some of the elements that are typically included in each act.

## FIRST ACT

In the first act, our hero will lose everything that's important to him and he will be forced into action. The first act is mostly falling action. We're going to learn a lot about the universe and the protagonist's big goal, but his life is going to get much, much worse.

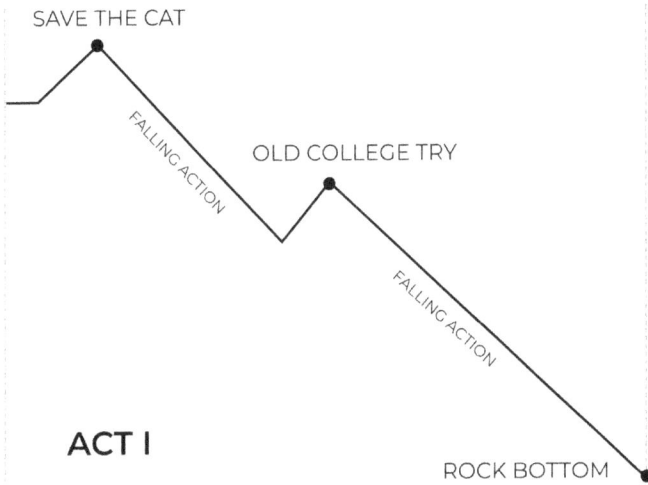

SAVE THE CAT

FALLING ACTION

OLD COLLEGE TRY

FALLING ACTION

ACT I

ROCK BOTTOM

## SAVE THE CAT

Before anything else can happen, though, we have to know who the hero is, and we have to know that he's a good guy.

Our first introduction to the protagonist is called the "Save the Cat" moment. The protagonist has to do something that shows the reader that he's good, decent, and/or moral. A good example would be for the protagonist to save a cat stranded in a tree, which is how this moment derives its name. While the event can be as dramatic as a feline rescue, it doesn't have to be.

Oftentimes, less is more for the Save the Cat moment. The protagonist just has to do something, anything, that your reader will say, "The world would be a better place if everybody did that."

Maybe the protagonist puts her shopping cart back in the corral, pushes a child on the swing set, or smiles at a stranger. Any small thing that allows the reader to say, "OK, this person is basically good." It's amazing how terrible you can make the protagonist after this and your readers will still like her, as long as the reader had a good first impression.

In *Star Wars*, we see Luke behaving politely to his aunt and uncle.

It's not a big deal, but we see that he's a good kid. When he talks to Uncle Owen about going to flight school, Luke ultimately respects his uncle's wishes.

Following the Save the Cat moment, as quickly as possible, the hero's world is going to unravel. Over the next 15,000-25,000 words, the hero will lose everything that's important to him.

This is sometimes called the "Inciting Incident," but that's too specific for me. Sometimes there is a really big event that kicks everything off—the mutants attack, the protagonist gets fired, or their house burns down. However, this isn't universal enough to insist on it. Even in *Star Wars*, which is by all accounts an action-driven story, there's a slow burn to the unraveling. R2D2 wanders off, which is a specific incident, but it's hardly an explosive moment. Instead, little things happen one at a time.

## THE OLD COLLEGE TRY

During this downward descent, the protagonist usually attempts an "Old College Try." The hero will make a half-hearted, unsuccessful attempt to correct his course and stop the hemorrhaging in his life. However, he'll only make things worse and the downward cycle of his life will continue.

Luke Skywalker attempts to rescue R2D2. If he had been successful, his life would have returned to normal and the unraveling would have stopped. He makes a valiant effort, but ultimately he's knocked out by the sand people, and has to be rescued by Obi-Wan Kenobi.

## THE ROCK BOTTOM MOMENT

Finally, after 15,000 to 25,000 words, which is one to three hours of reading time for the reader, we hit the "Rock Bottom" moment. The hero has lost everything that's important to him.

I want to clearly emphasize that the character has lost everything that's *important to him*. He may not have lost literally everything. If the protagonist cares about money only, then his money is gone. His family may be intact, but the money has disappeared.

For a different story, the opposite could be true. The protagonist has lost his family, the most important thing to him, but his wealth remains. As you develop your protagonist, make sure to determine what's truly important to him.

(Hint: oftentimes we're not honest with ourselves about what we value most, and the Rock Bottom moment can expose that. Double hint: This is a really good opportunity to develop theme and irony.)

Sometimes the hero does seem to lose *everything*.

In any case, we need the hero to be forced into a place where his only choice is to take action. Why? Because it's consistent with human psychology, and your reader will believe it.

In *Star Wars*, Luke's adopted family is murdered by the empire and left burning in the desert. He's lost everything that's important to him. He doesn't have a home any longer. All of his ties to his old life have been destroyed, so he has no choice but to accept Obi-Wan's invitation.

Humans don't naturally take the bull by the horns and turn their life around for no reason. We typically wait until things are so bad that we can't take it anymore. Recovered addicts talk about their Rock Bottom moment (which is where I derived the name).

Most addicts know they need to change for a long time, but they just don't do it. It's not until they hurt someone, humiliate themselves, or lose something important to them that they take action.

You know people who struggle with addiction. You know people who hate their jobs. You know people who are losing their marriages. You know people whose finances are a wreck. You see it, they see it, and any of those problems could be solved. But they're not going to change. Not until something dramatic happens. They're just going to keep showing up to the same life every day.

A reader won't believe that the protagonist just decides to take action for no reason. The protagonist has to hit Rock Bottom where his only choice is to give up and die (literally or metaphorically), or to fight back.

Of course the protagonist is going to rise up and fight back or we wouldn't have bothered to tell this story.

## SECOND ACT

In the second act, the protagonist is going to make his best effort to solve the problem. Unfortunately, he's going to fail, and he's going to make everything worse than ever before.

The first half of the second act is rising action as the protagonist rallies and fights back. The final half of the second act is falling action as the protagonist is beaten into a position that's more desperate than ever.

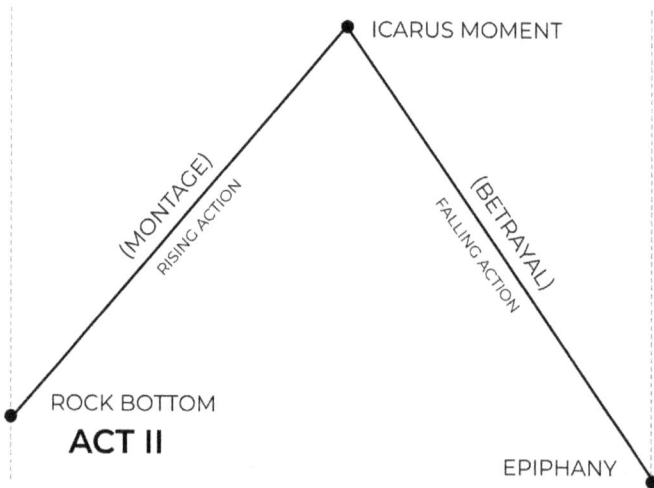

### THE MONTAGE

In the beginning of the second act, we're coming off of the Rock Bottom moment. The protagonist is stretching his wings for the first time and stepping into his destiny.

I call this section the "Montage," because in movies there's often a montage here. This is where the hero will do some training, he'll build a thing, or he'll start to investigate.

For about 10,000 words, our hero will be on a generally upward trajectory. He'll make real progress.

But he has one or two major problems.

First, he's probably pursuing the wrong solution. He really doesn't have enough experience to even know what to solve, so the hero is typically pursuing a false goal. Luke Skywalker, for instance, believes his mission is to deliver a message to Alderaan.

Second, the protagonist doesn't yet have what it takes. The protagonist hasn't assembled the full team of friends for the complete skill-set, or he hasn't yet learned the big lesson that will crack the problem wide open. In either case, our hero only has half of his bag of tricks. In *Star Wars*, Luke hasn't found his home among the Rebel Alliance, and he hasn't yet learned to trust his gifting with "the force."

In the second act of *Star Wars*, Luke believes that his mission is to help Obi-Wan deliver a message to the officials of the Republic at Alderaan. Along the way, he picks up a new friend, Han Solo, with his companion Chewbacca. On the journey, Luke gets some training. Obi-Wan begins to teach Luke about the force and teaches him to use the lightsaber. Things are all looking up.

There's a minor setback when the spaceship is captured by the Death Star. But what luck! That's exactly where Princess Leia is being held. In short order, the team kicks some butt, rescues the princess, and deactivates the tractor beam to prepare their escape. Everything is working out and it's all looking great!

However, in rescuing the princess, they raise the ire of Darth Vader, which brings us to our "Icarus Moment."

## THE ICARUS MOMENT

In Greek mythology, Icarus and his father were trapped on Crete. Icarus's father crafted wax wings so that they could fly off of the island and escape. Despite his father's warnings not to fly too high, Icarus flew too close to the sun, his wax wings melted (because that's how science works), and he plummeted into the sea and died.

About halfway through the second act, our hero will rise too high, and his fortunes will dramatically change. This is the Icarus Moment.

Oftentimes, the Icarus Moment occurs because the protagonist has made himself into a real threat to the bad guys. This is not always the case, but oftentimes in the first act the protagonist hasn't yet been singled out for special prejudice. In the first act, the protagonist is just sort of collateral damage, or in the wrong place at the wrong time.

Darth Vader isn't specifically out to get Luke in the first act of *Star Wars*, their fates just cross coincidentally. It's terrible for Luke, but Darth Vader has no special malice for him and isn't even aware that he's there. However, in the second act Luke fights back, and as a result Darth Vader becomes specifically aware of him. The temperature rises for Luke and his friends.

The Icarus Moment usually pairs a great triumph with a great tragedy in a one-two punch. Just when everything is perfect, boom, not anymore. We're combining an amazing victory with a terrible tragedy. We're mashing the best and worst things together.

Specifically in *Star Wars*, Luke has rescued Princess Leia. But the unthinkable happens before they can celebrate—Luke's new mentor and only real friend, Obi-Wan, is killed by Darth Vader on the Death Star!

All of Luke's positive trajectory was connected to Obi-Wan, and now it's gone. Luke flew too close to the sun, and now as a result he's lost everything once again.

By trying to fight and address the problem, the protagonist exposes himself. After roughly 10,000 words of success, some specific event will happen, and the hero's prospects for success will plummet.

## THE BETRAYAL

I call the downward leg of the second act the "Betrayal," because it's often characterized by a betrayal from someone close to the protagonist.

Once again the protagonist's life is going to get worse and worse. Things are going to fall apart. Important relationships will unravel, misunderstandings will rise, tools will break, and resources will dry up. Things are going to get really bad.

As Luke and friends fly away from the Death Star, something is amiss. The escape was too easy. The audience learns that the goons on the Death Star planted a tracking device. Before long, we learn that the

Death Star has followed them and is now orbiting the moon of the last remaining Rebel Alliance base.

As the romantic tension between Han and Leia percolates, she gives Luke an unconvincing kiss and injects complexity and friction into all the character's relationships.

Before Luke and the Rebel Alliance can take action, Han Solo takes his money and splits. He has debts to pay and no interest in a political cause. What a betrayal! Just when we thought he was coming around.

The second act ends on a real down note. Once again, things can't get any worse. Were all of the hero's efforts for nothing?

## THIRD ACT

Never fear, the Epiphany is here!

The third act is when it all comes together. The protagonist is going to learn a major lesson, step into his new identity, and kick some butt. While the protagonist will still experience complications and setbacks, the third act is all about rising action.

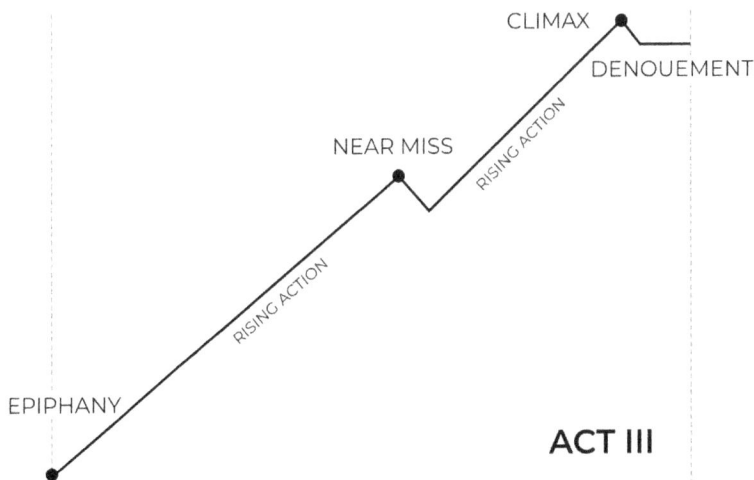

## The Epiphany

Just when all is lost, something clicks. The hero learns a lesson, finds a new tool, realizes how the evidence fits together, or finally assembles the whole team (almost). He finally understands what the real mission is, and the protagonist has what he needs to accomplish it. This is the "Epiphany."

Most of the time, the protagonist learned a lot from his false solution in the second act, and now he's ready to put the real plan in place.

In *Star Wars*, Luke Skywalker is invited to join the team of X-wing pilots. We see him welcomed into the mission briefing. Luke's internal struggle to step into his dream and his calling is fully realized, and he's surrounded by his tribe. This is a magical moment for Luke.

Oftentimes the Epiphany is as simple as a values lesson. If that's not the Epiphany itself, usually there's a values element that comes into play. The protagonist learns about teamwork or loyalty, for example.

This is where your theme and values really shine through. Even if the epiphany itself is a practical solution like how to blow up the Death Star, your choice to pair it with loyalty, duty, true love, or the grace of God will bring that value to roost for the reader.

But the book isn't over yet. Typically, the protagonist will spend another 20,000 words implementing the new solution.

## The Near Miss

Through the third act, the hero will be on a generally upward trajectory. However, about halfway to two-thirds of the way through this act, just when things were going so well, he'll encounter the "Near Miss."

It seemed like the plan was a slam dunk, but the Near Miss is when the solution falls apart, and final failure seems imminent.

As Luke attacks the Death Star with his new team, the plan is working. Their ships are too small for the Death Star's defenses and the bombers are moving into position to score the direct hit that will blow up the space station. Before that solution can come to pass, however, Darth Vader and his goon squad jump into their TIE fighters and absolutely tear the Rebel Alliance apart. Virtually no one is left but Luke and he's in poor shape. By all appearances the plan has failed and all hope is lost.

But don't worry, the hero will rally, continue on his way up, overcome the bad guy, and finally accomplish the major objective.

Oftentimes, the "Betrayal" from the second act is reversed in the Near Miss. The relationship that had broken down is fixed just in time to save the day.

In the case of *Star Wars*, Han Solo swoops in at the last moment before Luke's X-wing is destroyed, giving him the time he needs to take one final shot.

## THE CLIMAX

The resolution of the major conflict is called the "Climax." This is the moment that everything comes together. It's a short word, but a major scene. The Climax may have multiple parts, but there should always be a final scene of sudden and complete release. The "Aha" or "It is finished" moment.

The conflict with the antagonist (bad guy) can be resolved in one of two ways. Usually the bad guy is defeated, but sometimes he's converted from his wayward position and becomes an ally. In the case of some romance novels, the protagonist and antagonist even "fall in love."

In *Star Wars*, Darth Vader is knocked out of commission and goes hurtling into space before he can destroy Luke. Darth Vader is defeated. Luke is able to harness the power of the force and take the shot, which scores a direct hit and the Death Star explodes into a million pieces, presumably killing everyone inside.

Not all stories emphasize or resolve the external conflict, so it's possible the bad guy is just momentarily sidelined. There's no specific strategy that says how the big problem is resolved—the writer gets to be creative. However, some major conflict should be resolved. The reader should feel like the most important thing has been fixed.

## The Denouement

The Climax is followed by the "Denouement" which is pronounced like Day-New-Mah and is French for "Wrap it up." (It actually translates to "untie the knot.")

*Star Wars* wraps up the story with an awards ceremony, which is a very common element. Luke, Han, Chewie, and the droids receive medals from Princess Leia and what we can assume is the Alliance government.

The Denouement should be as short as possible. This is not the time to resolve every conflict that the novel introduced. That's not the way that life works, and with the exception of simplistic genres, doing so makes the book feel cheap. Loose ends are good.

Most stories will focus heavily on one particular conflict. The reader needs a release from the major conflict the story has been selling, but great books make the reader carry the weight of the book with them. Great books give the readers something to wonder about, and something to discuss with their book clubs.

## APPLYING RISING AND FALLING ACTION

The rising and falling action pertains specifically to the protagonist. Complex stories might have lots of things going on, so we're not talking about the overall feeling of positivity or negativity, we're talking about the protagonist's specific plight and outlook.

The rising and falling action refers to the order of events as they're presented in the novel or movie. When stories aren't told chronologically (the events are told out of order), the structure follows the story as it's told, not the original order of events.

For memoirs and creative non-fiction, a frequent strategy used to achieve the familiar three-act structure is to tell the events out of order so that the audience gets to the key moments in the right timing. For instance, the moment the big lesson was learned (a.k.a. the Epiphany) is placed at the beginning of the third act, about two-thirds of the way through the book, even if in the actual story it happened in the beginning.

As we've described this structure, rising and falling action happens over long periods of time. It's a general description of direction.

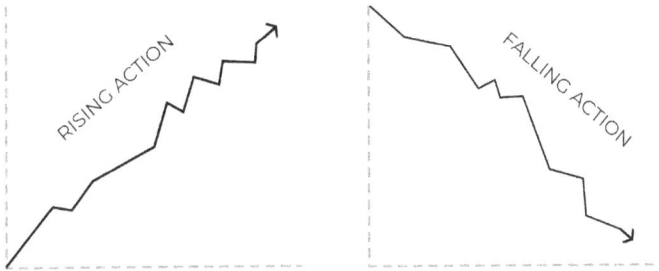

However, every section should have competing victories and setbacks. If we were to zoom in on any specific section it would be full of little ups and downs.

A roller coaster starts high and then you end at ground level. But you did a whole lot of up and down from beginning to end.

The named events, however, are specific. There should be an obvious point at which everything changes. At your Rock Bottom moment, for instance, things get really bad, but the character is going to make an obvious turn to begin pushing back.

Luke Skywalker didn't get gradually fed up and decide to leave town. His family was murdered and the moisture farm burned to the ground. A definitive moment in time was established.

## LENGTH OF THE ACTS

In many stories the three acts are almost exactly equal in length. A two-hour action movie will often hit the Rock Bottom moment at exactly forty minutes and the Epiphany at exactly eighty minutes. For a 60,000 word novel, plan for each act to be 20,000 words.

However, the most common deviation is to elongate the first act. This provides additional time to define the universe and develop the characters.

While the acts are theoretically equal in length, we see a fair amount of deviation in successful stories.

## STORIES OF AGENCY

"Agency" in story is a character's ability to take action on his own behalf. In the best stories, the main character usually feels stuck or trapped in the beginning of the story, but through the course of events he learns to take responsibility for his own actions and to determine his own destiny.

Most great stories are stories of agency. Through the first act the hero is seemingly trapped, but the audience knows that it's an illusion, and the only thing holding the hero back is himself.

Through the second act the hero will try to exert agency, but will be confronted by the full power of the system in which he's trapped and put back in his place. But in the third act, the hero will fully realize his own self-determination and define his own story.

Stories of agency are instantly relatable, even if we're not interested in the subject matter. We all know what it's like to feel trapped in a system, and we would all love to have the gumption to break out. We live vicariously through our heroes.

Because we relate so strongly to the helplessness of the hero, we'll watch stories of agency about nearly any subject. Agency supersedes our usual consideration of subject. We'll watch movies about football stars, piano players, dancers, and mathematicians, even though we typically maintain no interest in those subjects, because stories of agency resonate on a human level.

## CONFIRM IT:

The three-act structure is ubiquitous in our story-telling culture. It's one of your most valuable tools, because it instantly makes your story relatable on a human level.

A character is put in a bad situation and forced to take action, he tries to solve his problem but fails, then learns a lesson and tries again. That's your story. You've been that character in your own real life.

There are also areas of your real life right now where you'd like to get to act two and three. Maybe you even feel that way about writing a novel. Don't worry, you're holding your Epiphany Moment in your hands!

The three-act structure will take the guesswork out of your storytelling, so that you can move forward confidently, with an amazing, effective vehicle for your ideas.

To confirm this idea, watch one of the following movies and observe the three-act structure in action.

*Star Wars: A New Hope* (the original, aka "Episode 4", 1978)

*Iron Man 2* (2010)

*The Godfather* (1972)

*Hitch* (2005)

*Wonder Woman* (2017)

*Indiana Jones and the Raiders of the Lost Ark* (1981)

*It's a Wonderful Life* (1947)

*The Matrix* (1999)

*The Hunger Games* (2012)

Really you can watch just about any movie from a major studio produced in the last fifty years and you'll find this structure in effect. However, we'll use the movies in this list again and again through the book, so watching one of these will also help you understand future references. Plus, all of these examples are mapped out at NovelMatrix.com, so you can check your answers.

Use the provided worksheet to map out the story. You may need to watch the movie twice, especially if you haven't seen it before. The first time, just make a simple list of all of the major events and enjoy the story. The second time you watch it, try to pin those events to the appropriate places on the graph.

If you're struggling, use the clock to your advantage. Look up the running time of the movie and then divide by three—what big bad thing happens about a third of the way through? What big victory is coupled with a major setback about halfway through? Two-thirds of the way through, did the character learn a lesson or finally put the pieces together?

Compare your notes to the plans in the appendix of this book or at NovelMatrix.com. Did we come up with similar answers?

We often relate to the protagonist because the story is a story of agency. Ponder:

- In what ways was the story you watched a story of agency?

- In what ways was the main character "trapped" in the beginning of the story, literally or figuratively?

- Did the main character step up and take responsibility for her own life?

Take some time to really explore this and journal your answer.

# 5

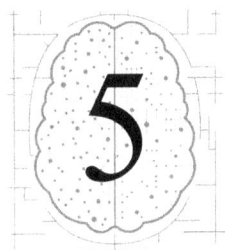

# FIVE CONFLICTS

DID YOU EVER make a diorama in school? It seemed like every year we had to make a pinhole diorama, where you'd poke a hole in one end of a shoe box and when you looked in, you could see some kind of historical scene inside.

Natural history museums love dioramas. You know the ones—cave men huddling around tinder as they try to create fire, or a bear frozen in place as if it's just snatched a trout out of a stream.

The key to a great diorama is the key to great conflict in a novel. We need enough elements to make it feel realistic, but not so many details that it lacks a clear focal point. A novel must feel like real life, but it can't actually capture the infinite complexity of real life. A novel is an intentional distillation of something real into something communicable.

If a story doesn't have a sufficient number of developed conflicts, it may feel hokey and contrived, even preachy. On the other end of the spectrum, too many conflicts leaves the reader feeling confused, unfocused, and with a really weak moment of release in the Climax.

Conflict is a key element of story. Just like the other ingredients, we need the right amount.

So how many conflicts should your story include? The answer is actually very easy: five.

## WHAT IS CONFLICT?

Remember this well: conflict, by definition, is two things in tension. Conflict occurs when two incompatible things occupy the same space at the same time. In order for it to be a real conflict, any progress on one side must come at the expense of the other side.

If a character wants something but there's nothing stopping him from getting it, it's not a conflict.

Luke Skywalker simply wanting to be a fighter pilot isn't a conflict. Even if he should pursue that and complete the necessary steps over a period of time, even if it's really hard for him, it's still not a conflict. It may be an obstacle, it may be a mission, it may be a struggle…but it's not a conflict.

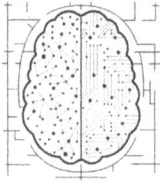

Conflict is two things in tension.

It becomes a conflict because his Uncle Owen tells him that he's not allowed to do it. Now it's an internal conflict because Luke wants two things at the same time. He wants to be a fighter pilot, but he also wants to please his uncle. It's impossible to do both things at the same time. He must choose one at the expense of the other. That's a conflict.

Luke blowing up the Death Star is not a conflict. It's a mission, it's an objective…but it's not conflict. It's just a good way to spend a Saturday night.

It becomes a conflict because Darth Vader intends to prevent Luke from blowing up the Death Star. Luke wants the Death Star to be destroyed, Darth Vader insists it must stay intact. It's impossible for both of them to have what they want at the same time. One will end happy and the other sad. That's a conflict.

A conflict is two things in tension. A challenge only becomes a conflict when there's an opposing force.

We will sometimes accept challenges in place of conflicts for true stories, but even that's a tough sell.

## TYPES OF CONFLICT

A character can engage in three types of conflict: internal, external, and philosophical.

**Internal conflicts** happen inside of the protagonist's head and heart. In order to be a conflict, there must be two things in tension.

Luke Skywalker wants to be a star fighter pilot, but he also wants to be obedient to his uncle. Those two ideas are in tension with each other, he can't do both at the same time. One must win to the exclusion of the other. The conflict is ultimately a decision that Luke has to make, it happens entirely inside of his head and heart, so it's an internal conflict.

**External conflicts** pit real, physical forces against one another. These forces don't have to physically fight but they must be real entities that express the conflict in the real world. For example, an employee versus their boss; or the leader of the rebels versus the leader of the empire.

Luke Skywalker is in direct physical battle with Darth Vader. This is an external conflict. The fate of the Death Star is a manifestation of that conflict that's happening. It's the touch point. They could be fighting over anything—a girl, a job, a competition—they happen to be fighting over a space station.

Even stories that are primarily focused on internal conflict must have an external component. We need some physical force in the universe that the protagonist must contend with.

The "bad guy" may simply represent what's bothering the protagonist. Perhaps it's a boss, who may be a super nice guy in his own right, but represents the forces that trap the protagonist in a life that he hates. We need that specific character on the page so that the reader can relate to the boss and see tangible outcomes in play.

**Philosophical conflicts** place ideas in opposition to one another. *What is right and wrong? How does the world work? What is our* *ethical duty to the people around us?* Typically secondary characters bring new ideas into the protagonist's life, and the protagonist must figure out how he'll view the world.

Han Solo believes that life is all chance, the best thing to do is to get what you can while you can. He's a hedonist. This is contrasted with Obi-Wan Kenobi, who believes that life is a matter of fate and it's our duty to step into our destiny. He's a Daoist. Luke Skywalker is caught between these two ideas. These two philosophies are in tension with each other and mutually exclusive. He must choose how he's going to live his life. He can't do both ideas at the same time. Ultimately, the story proves Obi-Wan Kenobi correct. In *Star Wars*, Daoism beats hedonism.

So we have three specific types of conflicts: internal, external, and philosophical. Great stories always explore all three.

## A TALE OF TWO WORLDS

It doesn't stop there, though. There's another layer of complexity to consider.

Three conflicts would be fine for a short story, but long-form stories like books and movies have two separate sets of the three types of conflicts—Little World conflicts and Big World conflicts.

Little World conflicts only really affect the protagonist. Big World conflicts affect society at large.

**Little World conflicts** only concern the protagonist. While there might be some collateral damage or a butterfly effect, the results of those conflicts only affect the hero.

Luke Skywalker wants to be a fighter pilot but his uncle said no. Since he is a good and loyal nephew, these two ideas exist in tension, so it's a real conflict. However, it starts and stops with Luke Skywalker. His resolution really doesn't have anything to do with anyone else. Luke Skywalker solving this problem won't affect systemic change in the universe (as far as we know).

**Big World conflicts** affect people groups and society at large. For example, the empire is terrorizing the planets in the galaxy and oppressing the citizenry. This is a big conflict, and if someone could fix it, it would have a lasting impact on large groups of people.

Successful long-form stories always include Little World conflicts layered over top of Big World conflicts.

This makes sense to you, because it's *how the world works*. In your life you have many problems that relate only to you. Your job, your car, your family.

While your choices impact a small circle of people, these conflicts really start and stop with you. After all, if you don't get the promotion at work, somebody else will. As far as society is concerned, the net result is the same—somebody's making more money and someone else stays the same. These are your "Little World" conflicts.

At the same time, you're also a member of certain groups that have some kind of conflict with other groups. Perhaps you identify strongly with a political party, a sports team, a religious group, or a cultural movement.

Most of these "Big World" conflicts you're involved in have relatively low stakes. You want your team to win the Super Bowl and another group wants their team to win. Either way, we'll all survive, but only one of you can win.

Whether First Baptist beats Downtown Presbyterian in this year's softball game probably won't echo into eternity.

But you may be part of groups that have a big impact. For instance, you may see yourself as part of the pro-life movement, which has the potential to impact the fate of almost a million unborn babies every year.

You may be a member of the military. Thereby your "group" has the power for tremendous good or evil in the world.

Regardless of your level of patriotism, you are a member of a nation. That nation has conflicts with other nations.

This is how the real world works. So we need a digestible representation of that in our story.

In *The Godfather*, Michael Corleone (Al Pacino) has to resolve his relationship with his family (a.k.a. the mafia). He has competing interests in tension. That's all about him, it's all his own little world.

If Michael can't get it sorted out and step into his role as head of the family, somebody else will. That's his Little World conflict.

However, that story is interwoven with a Big World conflict as the five crime families in New York are in an all-out war. It's Michael's family against the world. How that war shakes out will affect everybody in the region and potentially even the nation. That's a Big World conflict.

In *Wonder Woman*, Diana (Gal Gadot) has to resolve her personal sense of duty as an ancient warrior in modern warfare. That's unique to her. It starts and stops with her. It's her Little World.

Those personal struggles are layered over the big conflict of the Great War (World War I), which impacts everyone. That's the Big World.

In *Hitch*, Alex Hitchens has to figure out his complicated history with romantic relationships. He's carrying a lot of pain and frustration from his past and he has to choose to trust a woman again. All of that happens with just him—it's his Little World.

However, that personal turmoil is layered over this Big World tension between nice guys and jerks. There's a very real sense of these competing groups, and Hitch must use his talents (coupled with a dubious "the ends justify the means" philosophy) to help the nice guys overcome the jerks. The outcome of that battle has Big World results that could impact lots of people.

## TWO WORLDS, THREE CONFLICTS

Each of the three conflicts (internal, external, and philosophical) can be present in both the Big and Little World. We can identify them in great stories. They are always there.

The Little World will typically include all three types of conflicts.

- Our protagonist will be struggling with an internal conflict, often centered around his identity or sorting out his sense of duty.

- The protagonist will also have a direct adversary—an external conflict.

- The protagonist will be placed in the middle of a philosophical conflict, figuring out what's right and wrong.

In *Star Wars*, the Little World conflicts might look like this:

Internal: Luke's obligations to family versus Luke's personal dream to become a starfighter pilot

## LITTLE WORLD CONFLICTS

| INTERNAL | EXTERNAL | PHILOSOPHICAL |
|---|---|---|
| *TWO INCOMPATIBLE THINGS THE PROTAGONIST DESIRES* | *A DIRECT CONTEST WITH A NAMEABLE ENTITY* | *TWO OPPOSING WORLDVIEWS* |

External: Luke versus Darth Vader

Philosophical: Hedonism (Han Solo) versus Daoism (Obi-Wan)

## LITTLE WORLD CONFLICTS - *STAR WARS*

| INTERNAL | EXTERNAL | PHILOSOPHICAL |
|---|---|---|
| *PLEASE FAMILY VS BECOME A PILOT* | *LUKE SKYWALKER VS DARTH VADER* | *FULFILL DESTINY VS GET WHAT YOU CAN* |

The Big World will have its own set of conflicts. There typically isn't an internal conflict in the Big World. There's no single character to be "inside", but we do always have a Big World external conflict and a Big World philosophical conflict.

The external conflict is almost always two people groups pitted against each other. Again, this doesn't have to be a physical or violent altercation, it could be two political groups or even factions of the neighborhood association. But there are two distinct groups with interests that are in direct tension.

The Big World philosophical conflict will often relate directly to the two people groups. What are the opposing viewpoints?

In *Star Wars*, the Big World conflicts might look something like this:

## BIG WORLD CONFLICTS

| INTERNAL | EXTERNAL | PHILOSOPHICAL |
|---|---|---|
| X | TWO PEOPLE GROUPS IN CONFLICT | TWO IDEAS OF HOW THE WORLD OUGHT TO BE |

Internal: None
External: The empire versus The Rebel Alliance
Philosophical: Stability and order at all costs versus Freedom at all costs.

## BIG WORLD CONFLICTS - *STAR WARS*

| INTERNAL | EXTERNAL | PHILOSOPHICAL |
|---|---|---|
| X | EMPIRE VS REBEL ALLIANCE | STABILITY IS MOST IMPORTANT VS FREEDOM IS MOST IMPORTANT |

All together we have five active conflicts in every novel. This is the right number that satisfies readers. It's enough to provide the illusion of the vast, complex reality we live in, but few enough that a reader can keep track of and understand them.

It's important that all three types of conflicts are represented. We couldn't, for instance, have a bunch of external conflicts and just forget about the internal and philosophical conflicts. That story would be challenging to follow, and would lack emotional impact.

## LITTLE WORLD CONFLICTS

| INTERNAL | EXTERNAL | PHILOSOPHICAL |
|---|---|---|
| *TWO INCOMPATIBLE THINGS THE PROTAGONIST DESIRES* | *A DIRECT CONTEST WITH A NAMEABLE ENTITY* | *TWO OPPOSING WORLDVIEWS* |

## BIG WORLD CONFLICTS

| INTERNAL | EXTERNAL | PHILOSOPHICAL |
|---|---|---|
| X | *TWO PEOPLE GROUPS IN CONFLICT* | *TWO IDEAS OF HOW THE WORLD OUGHT TO BE* |

All of these conflicts will be present in a good story, but they won't all carry the same emphasis. Second to the universe, emphasis of conflicts will be one of the biggest factors in determining the genre of a story.

For example, adventure stories place a huge emphasis on the Little World external conflict (good guy versus bad guy). *Indiana Jones* is more about Indiana personally accomplishing his own cool thing than it is about saving the world, even though he'll also save the world.

Literary fiction often places the most emphasis on the Little World internal conflict. It's often about the main character resolving his own feelings or coming to terms with something.

Political thrillers often emphasize the Big World external conflict. For instance, the USA versus the USSR was a dominant theme in Tom Clancy's early work. Avoiding all-out global conflict was more important than the fate of the specific protagonist. If the protagonist died at the hands of the bad guy, but accomplished his mission to stop a nuclear war, it still felt like a win.

In any story, these five conflicts will not all resolve. In real life, your conflicts don't resolve all at once. Hopefully you get a big win here and there, but your other problems still remain.

Readers actually want some things to remain unresolved. If all the conflicts resolve, the story will often feel cheap and hokey.

Children's stories and Christmas stories often wrap up all the conflicts—everything gets tied up nicely with a bow. Because of the unique nature of those stories and our expectations, we'll stomach it, but we know it's cheap.

For most stories, the most important conflict will be resolved, and big progress will be made on one or two other conflicts, but the remainder of the five conflicts will not see progress or resolution.

In *Star Wars*, Luke defeats Darth Vader and blows up the Death Star. He also steps into his destiny, but he doesn't permanently save the universe or resolve any Big World conflicts. He only gives the oppressed people of the galaxy a temporary reprieve. The empire will continue to fight the Rebel Alliance. The war of stability versus freedom will continue to rage on.

In a planned trilogy, the protagonist will usually solve the Big World conflicts over the course of three books. The original *Star Wars* trilogy and *The Hunger Games* are great examples of this. In the first book, the hero will only overcome the Little World conflicts. By the end of the third book, each hero overcomes the Big World conflicts and achieves systemic change.

## CONFIRM IT:

Armed with the right number of conflicts, you'll engage your reader more effectively than ever before and also make sure that your book is saying something.

This conflict tool insists that you develop a contest between worldviews—it forces you to talk about something more than skin-deep.

To increase your awareness of this tool, watch a movie from our list and try to identify the major conflicts. For now, ignore the subplots and focus on the major issues the protagonist faces.

Conflicts are subject to your interpretation. Don't worry about getting the right answer. You and I may watch the same movie and come away with slightly different understandings or a different way to word the same thing. That's okay.

The conflicts all wash together in a long-form work—they marry in interesting ways. The important thing is to be able to pick out a primary internal, external, and philosophical conflict in the protagonist's Little World, and then to pick out an external and philosophical conflict in the Big World.

## A Brief Review

The Little World internal conflict is usually best stated as two things that the protagonist wants that are incompatible with each other.

The Little World external conflict is almost always the protagonist up against another person.

The Little World philosophical conflict is typically manifested by two supporting characters with different philosophical perspectives about the world. The protagonist is forced to choose between them. In the movie you choose to watch, look for two characters whose experience and worldview are intentionally contrasted. (Sometimes the protagonist already has a philosophy and only one character challenges it.)

The Big World external conflict is almost always two groups of people that are opposed to each other.

The Big World philosophical conflict draws into question what those two people groups represent. If you zoom out from the specific conflict, is there a question about fairness, justice, or good governance that's being asked? What's "just plain wrong" in this universe that needs to be sorted out?

Take the time to use the worksheet provided in the appendix and plot out the five conflicts. Don't worry about getting the right answer. This isn't high school and there's no test.

The important thing is to train your mind to begin experiencing story through the paradigm of story mechanics. As you begin to see the stories around you through these mechanisms, it will fundamentally change the way you understand your craft.

As you watch, ponder: how is your understanding of the story's message shaped by the way the creator defined and developed specific conflicts?

# 6

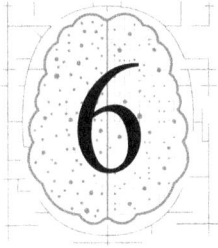

# SEVEN CHARACTERS

WE ALL NEED a little help from our friends.

Friendship is a major player in your overall success in life. According to a study by Flinders University, individuals with a strong friend group live on average 22% longer than those without confidantes.

Readers expect the protagonist to have help from his friends. That's *how the world works*.

There's rarely such a thing as a truly lone gunman. We may fall in love with a hero and they may occupy our memory when we reflect on a story, but stories almost always include a supporting cast. Stories that don't are usually boring and difficult to relate to, no matter how cool the hero is.

When I study novels, I divide characters into three classes: primary, secondary, and tertiary. The class determines the author's *duty to maintain* the character and your responsibility to develop backstory.

"Duty to maintain" simply means that the audience has an expectation that they'll get regular updates on the character. If a storyteller has a *duty to maintain* a character, the audience expects to know what happened to that character at the end of the story.

Some characters show up on the page and play their part, then they wander off. The audience may have some lingering curiosity about the character (and it may be the stuff of future fan-fiction!) but the audience really doesn't have any expectation that the story will ever revisit the cab driver, the bartender, or the hotel maid.

Great novels develop seven important characters. This includes the main character, some helpers, and some bad guys.

*Throughout the book I use him and her interchangeably. You'll find that especially obvious in this section. Naturally, any character can be either gender.*

## PRIMARY CHARACTERS

Stories really only have one primary character, and that's almost always our protagonist.

The word protagonist is derived from the Greek prefix "proto," meaning first, and the root word "agonist," which means hero or champion. When you put them together the word literally means "first hero."

It is possible to write a story in which the protagonist is not the main character, but this is uncommon. When we discuss story in the context of this book, the terms protagonist and main character are interchangeable.

The story has to maintain the protagonist, that's what we're here for. As readers, we expect to know where the protagonist is and what he's doing at all times. When the book ends, we deserve to know exactly what happened to the protagonist.

As readers, we also expect the protagonist to have a backstory. We want to know why and how she is the way that she is. If she can fly a plane, how? Why? If she's suffering from some past trauma, what happened? We want to know. We feel we *deserve* to know.

Oftentimes the protagonist is a kind of "everyman." The reader sees himself acting vicariously through the protagonist. In many books, movies, and TV shows, the protagonist is a sort of ordinary person who is thrust into a strange and extraordinary opportunity.

There are lots of examples of this vicarious everyman on modern television. Have you ever wondered what it would be like to become a criminal? You're a smart, capable, person. Could you do it? In *Breaking Bad,* Walter White, a mild-mannered high school teacher, becomes a drug kingpin and we can imagine ourselves in his shoes.

Or maybe you've wondered what it would be like to be some kind of high-powered professional. Perhaps if your life had taken a different turn. In *Suits*, Mike Ross is plucked from the streets and thrust into the life of a high-powered New York City corporate attorney. To varying degrees, we imagine ourselves as the character of Mike Ross.

The list goes on. Popular television will let you live as a member of a biker gang, any kind of detective you can imagine, a bounty hunter, a super wealthy housewife, or a famous musician.

But the protagonist need not be an everyman. In fact, the protagonist need not even be likable. Literature is peppered with memorable protagonists who are anything but "heroic." In the hands of an exceptional storyteller, the reader will connect with a protagonist who is downright despicable.

In most cases, the protagonist is the *only* dynamic character in the story. Every other character will be static. Your protagonist will make a huge change, but no one else will. Other characters may change their position or be convinced to make a different decision, but the nature of their mind and heart usually remain the same.

When we're discussing the narrative arc of a story and the three-act structure, we're exclusively talking about how it relates to the protagonist. Some stories have several characters that get a lot of page time. Nonetheless, one of those characters is the protagonist. In successful stories, usually only one of them is truly dynamic and follows the established story arc. The other characters will have their own arcs, but they don't fundamentally change.

*The Departed* is a great example of this[1]. Three characters dominate the story. Frank Costello (Jack Nicholson) is the crime boss, Colin

1. *The Departed* is a great example of certain types of storytelling. I've intentionally not included it in the list of recommended viewing because some of the content is very graphic. You may choose to watch it and consider the storytelling, consistent with your own conscience on the matter.

Sullivan (Matt Damon) is the wayward detective, and Billy Costigan (Leonardo DiCaprio) is the undercover agent. From a casual viewing, they all seem like "main characters." Each of the three gets a lot of screen time and has his own plot line. However, with a careful viewing, you'll see that Billy Costigan gets more screen time than the others, he follows exactly the established three-act arc, and he is dynamic—he is the only character who changes. Through his experience, he becomes a different person. The circumstances of the other characters change and they make different decisions accordingly, but their hearts remain the same, their priorities and ethos remain unchanged. Only Billy Costigan learns a lesson and becomes a new person.

## SECONDARY CHARACTERS - GOOD GUYS

The protagonist can't do everything himself. It's unbelievable. He needs a core cast of players that we'll call "secondary characters."

All of the secondary characters in a story carry a *duty to maintain*, but almost no responsibility to develop backstory.

At the end of the book, your reader will want to know how it turned out for the secondary characters. But these characters will bring skills, baggage, trauma, tools, and other resources, and the reader doesn't have the same questions about why and how.

Consider *Star Wars:* Luke's backstory, motivation, and skill set are consistently developed and explained. You know why he can do whatever he does. But everyone else—Obi-Wan, Han Solo, Princess Leia, R2D2—they just are whoever they say they are. The *Star Wars* franchise has made a lot of money developing these characters and their backstories in recent years, but as far as the original film is concerned, these characters just show up and we accept who they are and what they can do, with no explanation necessary.

The secondary characters we'll discuss here are not presented in order of importance. The function of each one is equally important, and must be present in the story.

The character archetypes your story must include are a guide, a sidekick, a frenemy, and an object of affection.

## GUIDE

The "guide" is a character who has typically walked the protagonist's path before him. The guide explains the universe for the reader's benefit and activates the protagonist on his mission.

The reader must trust the guide. The protagonist may choose not to take the guide's advice, but the guide is ultimately always right.

In *The Lion, the Witch, and the Wardrobe*, C.S. Lewis's Mr. Beaver described Aslan accordingly, "Course he isn't safe. But he's good." So it is with your guide.

The guide is good and good to the protagonist, but the protagonist's welfare may or may not be the guide's highest concern. Oftentimes the guide is loyal to a higher righteous cause, and he may send the protagonist on a tragic quest.

The guide must always give good advice and be essentially truthful (even if the truth may be cryptic). However, the protagonist does not always need to accept the guide's counsel. In fact, this is often the source of some of the protagonist's trouble. The audience is left to say, "You should have listened to the guide."

In many stories, the difference between the false solution of the second act and the real solution of the third act is simply that the protagonist has accepted the truth the guide offered in the beginning.

The guide is our only "relay" character, which means that his function can pass from one character to another. As long as the old guide is completely removed from the story (through death or other means), another character can step in to fill the role. However, there can only be one guide at any given time in the story. The old guide must be completely sidelined before the new guide enters the story.

Oftentimes, the guide does not contribute meaningfully to the protagonist's results. The guide can provide counsel, wisdom, and insight from afar, but rarely interacts directly in the mission.

Obi-Wan Kenobi is the guide in *Star Wars*. He helps Luke to understand the true nature of the universe. He literally explains out loud what the force is and how it works, all for the audience's benefit. He trains Luke to operate in this fictional universe and initiates Luke on his path. Ultimately, Obi-Wan helps Luke understand the true nature of his own identity, and he assigns Luke a specific quest accordingly.

Obi-Wan is a cool character, but his mechanical function is to explain this new universe to the audience and to point Luke in the right direction.

Other guides include Morpheus from *The Matrix*, Haymitch from *The Hunger Games*, and Marcus Brody from *Indiana Jones and the Raiders of the Lost Ark*.

The guide does not need to be a wise old man. The guide can come in many forms. However, there must be a trustworthy character to explain the fine rules of the universe and to help the protagonist understand her mission.

Oftentimes the guide dies in the first half of the story. This isn't necessary, but it does leave the protagonist in a do-or-die moment. The protagonist can no longer lean on the guide, she has to step into the mission on her own.

If the guide dies, we often see him return to the story in the third act in creative ways. The protagonist may simply recall the guide's counsel, or the protagonist may have a dream or supernatural experience to reconnect with the guide. In some cases, the function of the guide may be passed off to a new trustworthy character.

FUNCTION: The guide helps the reader to understand the universe and helps the protagonist to discover and accept her mission.

## SIDEKICK

If you want to get snooty, you can call the sidekick the deuteragonist. "Deutera-" is the Greek prefix meaning "second." (Like Deuteronomy, which is the *second* book of the law in the Bible.) So the sidekick is literally the "second hero."

The chief value of the sidekick is that he contributes skills to the protagonist. We don't expect the same level of backstory from the sidekick, which makes it much easier for him to contribute odd skills. For some reason, the reader just doesn't care as much.

Need someone who can fly a plane? Sidekick can do it. Need to hot-wire a car? Hack into a computer? Squeeze through a tiny crack? Isn't that convenient—the sidekick can do it.

The sidekick is fiercely loyal to the protagonist. He may make mistakes, but the reader should never question whether the sidekick is doing his best to help the protagonist. This is what differentiates the sidekick from every other secondary character. We always know that the sidekick is doing his best to serve the interests of the protagonist.

The sidekick can make an occasional mistake and can even be rejected for a time by the protagonist, but it should always be clear to the reader that the sidekick was doing his best. In a twist of irony, oftentimes a seeming mistake made by the sidekick will ultimately work out in the protagonist's favor.

This loyalty accomplishes two important things. It grounds the scene, providing an important emotional stability for the reader, and it also proves that your protagonist is fundamentally worth helping. If the protagonist were rejected, betrayed, and otherwise mistreated by *everyone,* eventually your reader will start wondering what the guy's deal really is.

You know that friend that you have that is always being mistreated and unjustly persecuted? Eventually the stories run a little thin. The sidekick solves this.

Because the sidekick is loyal to a fault, she also often becomes an honest sounding board for the protagonist. Your protagonist has thoughts in his head that your reader can't hear. The loyal sidekick provides someone for him to talk to out loud, so that your audience can get a peek inside.

R2D2 is the sidekick in *Star Wars.* Whenever Luke is in a jam that's beyond his capacity, R2D2 conveniently has exactly what's needed to fix it. Luke's trapped in a trash compactor? No problem, R2D2 will hack in and stop it. How does he know how to do that? He just does. How does he have the right mechanism to connect to the computer? He just does.

Did the little flappy thing break on the back of Luke's space ship? Good thing R2D2 is there to fix it. Did he always have a special mechanical arm that seems made for that specific job? Well I guess he did!

We never once wonder if R2D2 might be secretly working for the bad guys. He's solid as a rock.

Luke even expresses some of his internal thoughts to R2D2.

Sallah is our sidekick in *Indiana Jones and the Raiders of the Lost Ark*. Whatever Indy needs, Sallah can magically produce it. Access to the map room? He's got it. A bunch of guys to dig a hole? Check. Convenient exit from a tight jam at the bar? Sallah's on it! Camels? You know it's no problem!

How does Sallah get all of these things? We don't care. We never ask. We're just so thankful he did it in the nick of time!

Outside of an action and adventure scenario, your protagonist still needs lots of help. Romance, literary fiction—name the genre—your protagonist will need help, and it will be more believable if someone else provides it. Relationships, connections, money, skills…the list goes on, your protagonist will need things.

> FUNCTION: The sidekick provides tools and resources that the protagonist needs, and is unquestionably loyal to the protagonist. The sidekick is also a conversation partner to get the Protagonist's thoughts and motivations out of his head.

## FRENEMY

Not everybody can be fiercely loyal to the protagonist. That just wouldn't be any fun.

The frenemy introduces an instant variable to any scene. When he walks onto the page, we never know what might happen next. Things might get better or they might get worse.

Frenemies can be positive—they're basically loyal to the protagonist, but they're just such a screwup that they almost always make things worse (except for when it really counts). More commonly, frenemies are negative. We know they don't have any allegiance to the protagonist, but they have enormous potential to be helpful if only they had a heart (fortunately, they almost always will, just when all else seems lost).

Han Solo is the frenemy in *Star Wars*. He has no allegiance to anybody except himself. He'll help Luke for now…until somebody with a bigger purse shows up. But if only he would join the cause, he could be such a major asset! When it really counts, before the final battle, Han Solo loads up his cash and flies away. Classic Han! But wait, when all hope is lost and Luke is about to die, Han swoops in and saves Luke. We knew he'd do it!

Peeta from *The Hunger Games* is a perfect example of a positive frenemy. He's so devoted to Katniss that he complicates her life almost all the time. He loves her so much that he puts her in a position where she has to kill him. But he's not all bad. Sometimes, Peeta is the difference between life and death for Katniss.

FUNCTION: Introduce an unknown variable to the scene.

## OBJECT OF AFFECTION

The object of affection (or just "Object") is a character who needs saving. This character does not contribute meaningfully to the protagonist's success. The Object's relationship to the protagonist is typically good-natured (not always), but the protagonist will always give much more than he gets in this relationship.

Very simply, the object of affection gets in trouble and needs saving.

When I first developed early versions of the Novel Matrix, I named this character the "love interest," because that's the classic role. But that's too narrow. The protagonist usually has an affection or irrational loyalty to this character, but that interest does not need to be romantic.

The object of affection serves as a catalyst for the plot. When the protagonist needs to be spurred on to action, or to overcome a reservation, the object of affection will find herself in trouble and motivate the protagonist to action.

This is very important: the Object does not contribute meaningfully to the protagonist's success. If the sidekick always makes things easier and gets the protagonist out of a jam, the Object does the exact opposite. The Object gets the protagonist into the jam and constantly makes things harder. When we see the Object in the scene, it's cause for alarm.

In *Star Wars*, Princess Leia is a classic object of affection. Luke sees her in the holographic projection and he's catalyzed to action. Whenever Luke has an opportunity to stop and turn around, he's re-motivated by his attraction to her.

Notably, Princess Leia contributes no skills, tools, or other practical resources to the plot. She may pick up a blaster now and then, but by and large she is dead weight. She is in need of constant saving. She is baggage, in every sense of the term.

But, as previously mentioned, the object of affection does not need to be a romantic interest.

In *The Hunger Games*, Katniss is catalyzed to action by her little sister Primrose. In both a literal and figurative sense, Katniss fights for Primrose. Primrose doesn't help Katniss survive in any way, aside from moral support, but she is the direct cause of the trouble.

In *Gone in 60 Seconds,* Memphis Raines's (Nicolas Cage) little brother Kip is threatened by the bad guys, so Memphis breaks his oath to never again steal cars. Without the object of affection, Memphis would have said no to the big car heist and happily returned to his straight life. Kip doesn't bring any special skills to the crew. From a functional standpoint he could be easily removed or replaced, except that no one else could motivate Memphis to do stupid things like Kip does.

The object of affection is an effective tool to bring the protagonist into direct confrontation with the bad guys. In many stories, the protagonist could have simply avoided the bad guys and accomplished his mission, but instead he has to go into the lion's den in order to rescue the object of affection.

FUNCTION: The object of affection catalyzes the protagonist to action. This character keeps the protagonist moving forward, often motivating the protagonist to take risks when he could otherwise just walk away, and often bringing the protagonist into direct conflict with the bad guys.

## THE GOOD GUYS

| ARCHETYPE | FUNCTION | EXAMPLES |
|---|---|---|
| GUIDE | 1. EXPLAINS THE UNIVERSE<br>2. ESTABLISHES THE PROTAGONIST'S MISSION | 1. OBI-WAN KENOBI<br>2. MARCUS BRODY<br>3. MORPHEUS |
| SIDEKICK | 1. PROVIDES TOOLS, SKILLS, AND RESOURCES<br>2. ESTABLISHES LIKEABILITY | 1. R2D2<br>2. SALLAH<br>3. TOM HAGEN |
| FRENEMY | 1. INJECTS A VARIABLE INTO THE SCENE<br>2. MAY BE POS. OR NEG. | 1. HAN SOLO<br>2. PEETA<br>3. CAPTAIN RHODES |
| OBJECT OF AFFECTION | 1. CATALYZES THE PROTAGONIST TO ACTION<br>2. IS NEVER HELPFUL | 1. PRINCESS LEIA<br>2. PRIMROSE<br>3. UNCLE BILLY |

# SECONDARY CHARACTERS - BAD GUYS

Every story has bad guys—no exceptions. The bad guys aren't always evil—twirling their mustaches in dark corners—but we must have someone that stands opposite to the protagonist.

In literary fiction, the bad guy might actually be a decent person, but he embodies and represents the internal conflict the protagonist faces. Perhaps it's the manager at the coffee shop, the landlord, the smothering parent, or the other suitor. The bad guy might even be a kind person, but he symbolically represents bondage, insecurity, or some other internal issue of the protagonist.

We call this a "representative" antagonist. The character isn't necessarily bad, he or she is just an unfortunate cog in the system as it relates to the protagonist.

But of course most stories, even literary fiction, have real bad guys. A story is based on a character who wants something, and somebody has to stand in his way. Sometimes these bad guys are just plain evil, absolutely rotten, no-good individuals, or sometimes they're as much a victim of circumstance as anybody else.

In literature we call the bad guy the **antagonist**, which comes from the Greek prefix "anta-," meaning against. The antagonist is literally "opposed to the hero".

Great stories will have two sets of conflicts, a Big World and a Little World, which means that there will typically be two bad guys. In most stories, we'll find an antagonist for the "Little World" to be directly opposed to the protagonist. We'll also find a **mega-antagonist**, a really really bad guy who represents the Big World conflicts.

## ANTAGONIST

The antagonist stands directly opposed to the protagonist. He is there to make the hero's life miserable. In some cases, the protagonist and antagonist are competing for the same thing, like Indiana Jones and Belloq in *Raiders of the Lost Ark*. Other times, the antagonist simply doesn't want the protagonist to achieve his goal, like Darth Vader wants to stop Luke in *Star Wars*.

The antagonist is often a victim of the system. Is Darth Vader a bad guy? Well, yes, he is. But he's also a victim of the emperor's sorcery and manipulation.

In *The Hunger Games*, Cato is a real jerk, big time. But he's also a victim of the system, forced to fight in the Hunger Games just like Katniss.

Sometimes the antagonist is just a plain old bad dude. One of the things I love about many of Clive Cussler's novels is that he doesn't make any excuses for the bad guys. Good guys are good and bad guys are just plain bad.

Antagonists are easy to pick out. Who does the protagonist have to defeat to get what he wants?

Sometimes the antagonist appears to be a group. However, if we watch carefully, we'll see that effective storytellers will spotlight one member of the group to represent the group as a whole. In *The Hunger Games*, Cato is the antagonist. Even though Katniss is technically fighting against twenty-three other tributes, Cato ultimately stands in her way and represents the group through the story. We barely know the names of most of the other contenders Katniss faces.

FUNCTION: The antagonist stands opposed to the protagonist's personal success. Sometimes this is in direct opposition, sometimes the antagonist is in competition for the same thing, and sometimes the antagonist simply manifests the character's internal struggle or insecurities.

## MEGA-ANTAGONIST

The mega-antagonist (MA) is usually just plain evil. He's rotten, no-good. The MA typically represents everything that is wrong with the universe of the story.

If the protagonist defeats the regular old antagonist, a new bad guy will rise up in his place. Defeating the MA, however, would result in real systemic change.

Katniss defeats Cato in *The Hunger Games*, only to find a whole new crop of bad guys in the "Quarter Quell" of the second book. But if she defeats President Snow, the master of the whole system, then things will really change and the cycle will stop. President Snow is the mega-antagonist.

When Luke Skywalker defeats Darth Vader and blows up the Death Star, it's only a temporary victory. There will be a new, bigger Death Star right behind it. Darth Vader conveniently returns in the second movie, but if he didn't, no doubt the emperor would have another ambitious Sith Lord waiting to stand in Luke's way. However, when the emperor is destroyed, the galaxy can rejoice.

Mega-antagonists come in all shapes and sizes, but it should be a real, singular person. It can't be an idea or a construct, we need a specific person that we can name, even if that character is obviously symbolic of a specific idea. If there's a group behind something, like a secret society orchestrating a conspiracy, you still need to pick one guy that's the head of the snake.

In *Raiders of the Lost Ark*, the Nazis as a whole are really the overwhelming force of evil in the story's universe. However, we have a specific focal point in Major Arnold Toht (the slithery Nazi guy played by Ronald Lacey) who is a singular representative of the Nazis throughout the story.

In *The Godfather*, even though we have a whole committee of crime families that really embody the Big World conflict, Barzini rises to the front as the clear "head of the snake."

The antagonist and MA don't usually work alone. Just like the protagonist, they have their own crews and henchmen, which are tertiary characters.

FUNCTION: The mega-antagonist (MA) represents everything that is truly evil in the world. If the MA were to be defeated, real systemic change would result.

## THE BAD GUYS

| ARCHETYPE | FUNCTION | EXAMPLES |
|---|---|---|
| ANTAGONIST | 1. DIRECTLY OPPOSES PROTAGONIST 2. OFTEN A VICTIM OF THE SYSTEM | 1. DARTH VADER 2. DR. RENE BELLOQ 3. CATO |
| MEGA-ANTAGONIST | 1. REPRESENTS EVERYTHING WRONG WITH THE UNIVERSE 2. JUST PLAIN EVIL | 1. THE EMPEROR 2. PRESIDENT SNOW 3. MR. POTTER |

# TERTIARY CHARACTERS

The seven important characters are the protagonist, guide, side-kick, frenemy, object of affection, antagonist, and mega-antagonist. A great story will maintain all of these characters throughout the story—we'll know where their stories end.

But your story will also be full of other people.

Tertiary simply means "of third importance." It comes after primary and secondary.

Story worlds are full of tertiary characters. The protagonist will usually interact with lots of different people through the course of a long and complex story. However, these are tertiary characters because the reader has no expectation that the storyteller will maintain them or develop their backstories.

Tertiary characters walk onto the page. Your reader believes they are who they say they are. Then they walk off. The reader will pay them little mind.

Tertiary characters are usually perfunctory characters. They perform some practical function of the plot—taxi drivers, bartenders, waiters, stewardesses, even old friends.

Henchman are tertiary characters that play a big part in the plot of the book. We can use the word "henchman" in reference to any of the antagonist's or mega-antagonist's helpers, even if they're not literal henchman in the action/adventure sense.

Even if the henchmen are very cool, they're usually not developed as characters.

In *Star Wars*, stormtroopers just show up and die. Even Luke's fellow X-Wing pilots just die and we move on. These characters have no backstory and no resolution. Some of them even have cool lines, but then they're gone.

On the Death Star, there are a variety of officers. Some of them are important to the plot. Ultimately, they serve to show us the character of Darth Vader. We assume they all die, but the audience doesn't really care about the specifics.

Indiana Jones kills loads of Nazis. Remember when he fights the big bad dude in front of the airplane in *Raiders of the Lost Ark*? If you've seen it, you remember it! It's an iconic scene. Who was that guy? We don't know, and we don't care.

It was a really cool, elaborate scene. The muscle head is critical to that scene. Nonetheless, he shows up, we know nothing about him except that he's a big goon, and then he blows away on the wind (literally). He doesn't even have a name.

In *The Hunger Games*, every single tribute is important in an ethical sense (dying children and all). But by and large, we know next to nothing about any of them. Each one plays his or her minor part and then they're gone. Most of them we really don't even know how or when they die.

## FORM FOLLOWS FUNCTION

The three act structure and the five conflicts are rock solid. You're

## COMPLETE CHARACTER FUNCTIONS

| ARCHETYPE | FUNCTION |
|---|---|
| GUIDE | 1. EXPLAINS THE UNIVERSE<br>2. ESTABLISHES THE PROTAGONIST'S MISSION |
| SIDEKICK | 1. PROVIDES TOOLS, SKILLS, AND RESOURCES<br>2. ESTABLISHES LIKEABILITY |
| FRENEMY | 1. INJECTS A VARIABLE INTO THE SCENE<br>2. MAY BE POS. OR NEG. |
| OBJECT OF AFFECTION | 1. CATALYZES THE PROTAGONIST TO ACTION<br>2. IS NEVER HELPFUL |
| ANTAGONIST | 1. DIRECTLY OPPOSES PROTAGONIST<br>2. OFTEN A VICTIM OF THE SYSTEM |
| MEGA-ANTAGONIST | 1. REPRESENTS EVERYTHING WRONG WITH THE UNIVERSE<br>2. JUST PLAIN EVIL |

going to find these elements exactly as we've described them in practically all of the most successful stories in our culture. The secondary characters, however, have a little more variability.

Many stories will use exactly the six secondary characters that we've outlined here. Some stories, however, will play mix and match for interesting results.

Secondary character types are more about function than archetype.

Each character type serves a function. Each type is specifically designed to bring certain assets to the story.

Here's an abbreviated function of each:

GUIDE: Establishes the universe and assigns the mission.

SIDEKICK: Provides skills and resources to the protagonist.

FRENEMY: Introduces a variable to the scene.

OBJECT OF AFFECTION: Catalyzes the protagonist to action.

ANTAGONIST: Directly embodies the conflict or resists the protagonist.

MEGA-ANTAGONIST: Embodies everything that is just plain wrong with the universe.

Not all stories include every character listed here, but most do, because the function is important to the story.

What's important is that all six secondary character *functions* are represented in a story.

For instance, we may not have a character that is only an object of affection, but every story needs a character who will consistently inspire the protagonist to do crazy things. A great storyteller may be able to find a creative way to combine that function with another character in the list, but the function must be present.

There are a few common combinations we see, but this is an opportunity for an enterprising writer to make new combinations work.

Combining the guide and the object of affection is a natural fit. Neither the guide nor the Object typically contribute directly to the protagonist's success, so there's no problem when we combine the archetypes.

Morpheus in *The Matrix* is this type of character. He functions as both the guide and the object of affection. He's the perfect guide. Morpheus is first and foremost trustworthy, his highest commitment is to the cause, and he literally explains the rules of the universe. But he is also the object of affection.

Morpheus does not contribute materially to the plot (everyone else does all of the action), all Morpheus ever does is get in trouble, get captured, and need saved, which always catalyzes Neo to action. Morpheus loses every fight he's a participant in. One character can serve both *functions*.

*The Matrix* is also an example of a story in which the protagonist's romantic interest is not the object of affection. Trinity is Neo's sidekick, unwaveringly loyal and bringing necessary skills, and also the romantic interest.

Some character types cannot be combined. For instance, a character could not be both the sidekick and the frenemy. The function of the sidekick is to be loyal to a fault and always help the protagonist, while the function of the frenemy is to have questionable loyalty and to only sometimes help. No character could be both at the same time. It's incompatible.

In the right circumstances, the guide can be a frenemy, because the guide is loyal to his cause, not the protagonist.

Positive and negative characters can also be combined. The antagonist can be the object of affection. This is often a feature of romances and adventure stories alike.

| | GUIDE | SIDEKICK | FRENEMY | OBJECT | ANTAGONIST | MEGA-A |
|---|---|---|---|---|---|---|
| GUIDE | | | ✓ | ✓ | | |
| SIDEKICK | | | | | | |
| FRENEMY | ✓ | | | | | |
| OBJECT | ✓ | | | | ✓ | |
| ANTAGONIST | | | | ✓ | | |
| MEGA-A | | | | | | |

**LIKELY CHARACTER COMBOS**

Most readers couldn't name these character archetypes, but they do know the functions. It's part of *how the world works*. They'll feel it if they're missing.

As readers, we fall in love with characters. If we can relate to a character and understand what's at stake, we'll stick with stories through a lot of bad writing and poor story structure.

With this cast of character archetypes in hand, you hold the power to hook into your readers' hearts and to help them understand the motivations of your protagonist at a much deeper level.

## CONFIRM IT:

Do you have a guide, a frenemy, a sidekick, or an object of affection in your life? What about an antagonist? Is there a mega-antagonist (perhaps a politician) that you feel embodies everything wrong with the world?

These character functions work in stories because they're similar to how we understand our own lives, albeit a simplified version.

Watch a movie from our list and identify the primary and secondary characters.

The character list is where we see the most variability, but remember that the functions are very important. If you can't identify the exact archetypes, who is fulfilling each function? Are any of the character functions combined?

Who is catalyzing the protagonist to action, and really not contributing much to the team?

Who sometimes acts in the protagonist's favor, but is just as likely to willingly or mistakenly ruin everything?

Which character said things out loud that you needed to know in order to understand the universe? Did this character also help the protagonist to define his goal?

# 7

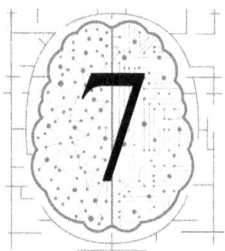

# THE GREATEST STORY EVER TOLD

NO DISCUSSION OF STORY would be complete without some exploration of the best-selling book of all time. It's a story that has resonated with readers across cultures and translations.

This book has sold more than five billion copies, has been translated into more than 3,500 languages, and has weekly fan clubs that meet on every continent on earth (yes, even Antarctica).

That book is the Bible.

While the way the Bible came to be a book is different from many other books, it is a book nonetheless, and it is a story. Approximately thirty-five different authors contributed to the Bible, many of them with limited or no awareness of the other writers. Together, they created one comprehensive, interwoven story, which is miraculous in itself.

Can you imagine writing a book with thirty-four other writers, with no instructions, no editor managing the project, and no ability to communicate with the other writers, yet producing a book with no substantial contradictions?

Countless works of fiction have borrowed, adapted, and allegorized biblical narratives and themes. Our greatest works of literature, even those that disagree with the premise of the Bible, allude to this best-selling book.

The Bible is a love story. It's a complex story with some parts that are hard to understand, but the themes are simple. It's about someone who loves someone else, is separated from the person he loves, and wants to be reconciled. Through a huge personal sacrifice, that reconciliation is made possible so that the lovers can reunite.

The Bible proves that the story arc and many elements of the Novel Matrix are hardwired into the universe.

The Bible is the story of God and his passionate love for the people He created. The protagonist is a character named Man.

There is a mega-antagonist named satan.

In the beginning, God created the heavens and the Earth, and it was good. Man was good and he lived in perfect harmony with God in a home called Eden. This is the Save the Cat moment.

God taught Man but also gave him freedom and autonomy, even allowing Man to name all of the creatures that God had made. God loved Man and made him with an innate capacity to crave God's love and attention, and God gave his love to Man in abundance. It was very good.

Only it didn't stay good. We don't know if it was hundreds, or thousands, or even billions of years that Man lived with God in Eden. The antagonist showed up though, and Man's story arc went into steep decline. Satan enticed Man to break his alliance with God, and make an alliance with him instead.

Because of these choices, Man was cut off from God, and all future generations with him. Man was no longer able to interact with God like he had in Eden. This thing that Man was made to do more than anything else, to love God and be loved by Him, became impossible.

Through Genesis, the first book of the Bible, Man's story only grew worse. He became further and further separated from God. Man tried to fulfill his missing God-love by serving his own selfish interests, lusting after his own pleasures, and hurting other people.

There was an Old College Try, though—a first effort at reconciling the broken relationship between God and Man. Around 1,800 BC, God gave Man a covenant through a man named Abraham, promising that he would make a way for Man to be fully reconciled to God one day.

Nonetheless, like most stories, things continued to get worse and the downward story arc persisted. Famine, wickedness, betrayal... Until finally, the Israelites, the descendants of Abraham who are called God's chosen people, were enslaved in Egypt for 400 years.

It really couldn't get any worse. The Egyptian Pharoah started killing all of their babies. Unless something happened, all would be lost. Despite the promise that they carried from God for Man, Israel was at its Rock Bottom moment. Something had to change or this would be the end of the story.

But something happened indeed! To begin the second act of the story, around 1290 BC, God raised up a man named Moses as a prophet, and through mighty miracles he freed Israel from the tyranny of Egyptian bondage. Moses led Israel to "The Promised Land," where all of their problems would be solved.

The next part of the story has its own ups and downs, but is an upward story arc. Gradually Israel found its way to the Promised Land. A new civilization was founded, based on the instructions Israel had received from God through Moses. Little by little, things were looking up.

Things were really bright as King David took the throne of Israel around 1,000 BC and walked in the authority of God. His son Solomon built a temple for God around 957 BC and the fiery presence of God came to inhabit it! Solomon's empire was unlike any other, and kings came from afar not only for his wealth but for his wisdom.

Surely this nearly perfect civilization was what God had meant when he promised Abraham that Man would be reconciled forever through Israel.

If it was possible to re-establish God's Eden on Earth through human efforts, this magnificent dynasty in Israel had achieved it. This is the Icarus Moment of the Bible.

But as in so many stories, their great success was also their downfall. Israel didn't use their success to pursue perfect union with God. Instead, satan distracted them with greed, earthly pleasures, and temptations.

As perfect as it may have seemed for a moment, for the next 900 years, this once mighty Hebrew civilization fought against division, rebellion, and idolatry. For the next 900 years, they were plagued by this curse and fell deeper and deeper into despair.

A series of kings took David's throne, one after another, and with each one the glory of the Kingdom declined. Some kings were good and some were bad, but little by little everything that David and Solomon achieved was destroyed. Without God's help, Israel's empire was repeatedly overrun.

Finally, the Israelites were crushed by the Babylonians. The capital city of Jerusalem was left in absolute ruins and the temple Solomon had built was destroyed.

In this time prophets like Isaiah and Jeremiah heard from God and offered hope and reminded Israel of the promise God had given Abraham, but year after year, century after century, no relief arrived.

Two men named Ezra and Nehemiah finally rebuilt Jerusalem, but the glory of God was never restored. They built a new temple and waited for God to come in his fiery presence and fill it like he had done for Solomon, but God never came. They had fallen farther than ever before from being reconciled to God.

All hope was lost. The Kingdom had fallen and the Israelites were slaves to one tyrannical master after another.

For 400 years, the story was silent. Nothing to report.

When the story of the Bible picks up again with the third act, the Israelites were under Roman rule, just another oppressive outside force. They had simply traded one tyrant for another.

But behold, a light dawned! The great Epiphany was about to be made known! God made himself human and came to Earth as a child named Jesus, marrying heaven and earth together as God in a human body. Jesus was born to Mary, a virgin, in the most humble of settings. But even so, kings came from far away to worship him.

And things were amazing. Jesus smashed through barriers, banishing sickness and demons everywhere he went, providing for those who had nothing. Could God's promise to Abraham finally be fulfilled?

Jesus's popularity swelled. While his ministry was criticized by the religious people of his day, he was largely respected by the common folk, and thousands would come to hear him teach wherever he went. Everyone he touched was healed of sickness and disease, and no one had heard teaching like his before—calling the people to change their hearts.

Finally, Jesus entered Jerusalem. The people celebrated and compared Jesus to the great King David. This was it! The moment they'd been waiting for. They were sure that Jesus would now take up Israel's authority, banish Rome from Jerusalem, and restore the Israelite empire like David and Solomon! This time it would last forever, like the prophecies had said. The Climax was within reach!

But just when things were going so well, the religious leaders stirred up the people. The crowds turned on Jesus. The religious leaders manipulated the government to have Jesus executed.

His disciples looked on as Jesus was brutally tortured and hung on a cross. The mighty one who was going to restore Man to God breathed his last and died. Surely this was the end, all was lost. Jesus's disciples knew that he was really dead, and they believed that was the end. Was it all a big mistake?

But Jesus wins. It was only a Near Miss because Jesus was restored to life under his own power. As it turns out, he was different than any human man—Jesus had power even over his own death.

In a moment, Jesus reframed all of the prophecies. He provided a new way to understand the things God had said and the pieces finally fit together.

Finally, it all made sense! The foreshadowing was there, God had been telling us how he would do it the whole time. We just didn't know how to listen. Jesus provided the key.

Jesus conquered death, rose from the grave, and took all spiritual authority over the universe. The world is more than what we can see, touch, and hear. In fact, those aren't even the most important parts!

Jesus ascended to God's throne in Heaven to begin an empire of a heavenly type. Solomon's earthly empire at the peak of the second act was a false mission, God had always intended a spiritual empire, not a physical one.

God didn't intend to make a country rule over all of the others in order to facilitate his reconciliation with Man. Instead, He made a way for each individual to choose to be personally reconciled to God.

Now Jesus reigns in Heaven alongside Father God, while his enemies are placed under his feet. He has made a way for all of Man to be reconciled to God right now. Each individual has the power to accept Jesus as Lord and resume the connection with him that God intended in the Garden of Eden.

What a glorious era that we live in! The story isn't done yet. In the coming Climax, all of Heaven and Earth will declare the Kingship of Jesus. The Bible tells us that every knee will bow before Him.

But the story of the Bible is incomplete. Every tongue, tribe, and nation will be given an opportunity to turn to Jesus before the Climax. But Jesus promised that the Climax could happen at any time.

Those that choose Jesus will have an enduring, never-ending Denouement in a new, perfect Earth, basking in the light of the Father for all eternity.

This is the story of the universe! This is the story of our creator, clambering to reclaim His creation.

The book of Revelation compares the Church, which includes all of the people who profess a belief in Jesus as God, to a bride. This is the story of a love that was lost but has been found.

The whole universe cries out with the structure that we've decoded. As it turns out, we are telling the only story!

The Bible, as a comprehensive story assembled from more than thirty authors, has a Save the Cat, an Old College Try, a Rock Bottom, an Icarus Moment, a great EPIPHANY, and a Near Miss! Billions of people around the globe gather regularly to celebrate the coming Climax.

Isn't that nifty?

Whether you believe it or not, based on five billion copies sold, I'd say it's a pretty compelling story, and it's worth learning from.

THE NOVEL MATRIX

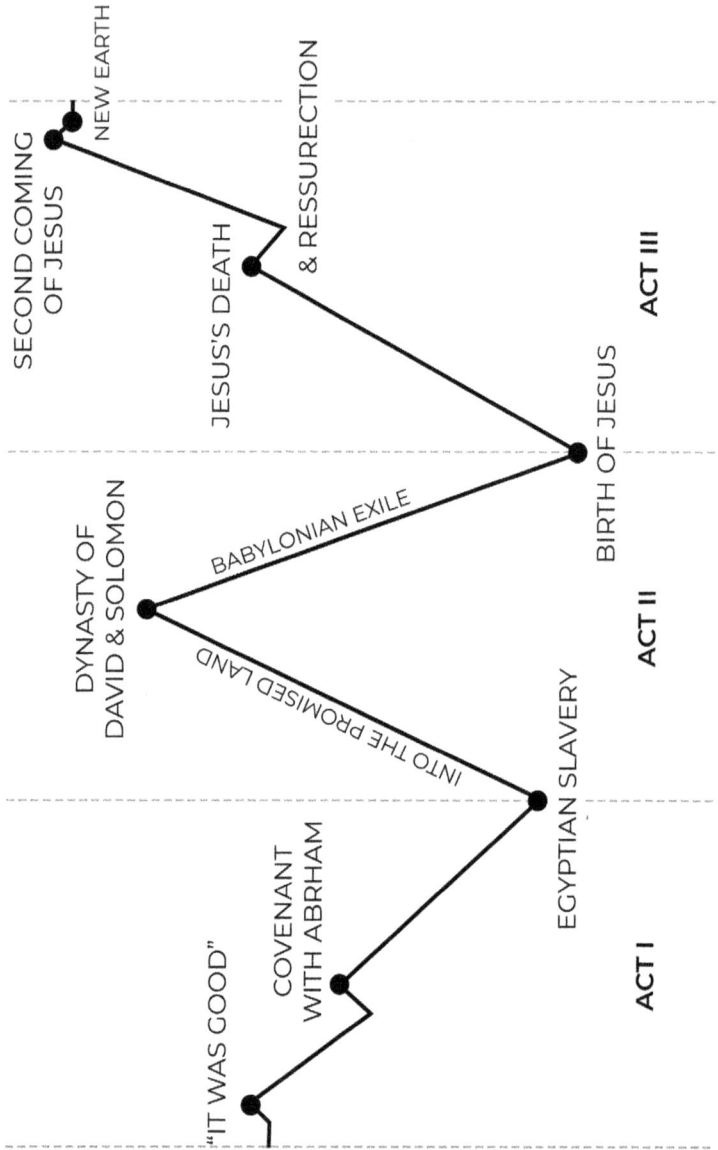

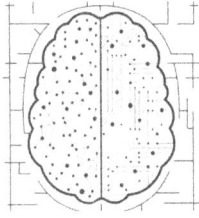

The Novel Matrix is everywhere. It is all around us. You see it when you go to church, when you visit the library, and when you turn on the television. (OK, so I may have borrowed this from Morpheus.)

Long-form storytelling, like a novel, has certain conventions that have to be followed.

Great stories have a well-defined universe, a plot structure with a defined beginning, middle, and end, five developed conflicts, and usually seven critical characters. We haven't yet discussed *how to write a novel,* this is just *what a novel is.*

These elements satisfy how we understand stories and what we intuitively know in our hearts of *how the world works*, and these elements conform to our own human psychology. When these ingredients are in place, it just feels right.

It doesn't matter what genre the story is, it doesn't matter what narrative style—these are just the things great stories do.

There are exceptions. There are exceptions to most rules. Of course there are successful stories that defy what we've discussed here. But overwhelmingly, modern literature and film confirms that these storytelling principles are sound.

As a developmental editor, I give every story a chance. If the story works, I don't care if it follows the Novel Matrix. But time and time again, when something about the story just isn't connecting, it's solved by applying the principles we've observed here.

In Part II, we'll walk through how to apply the Novel Matrix to your project.

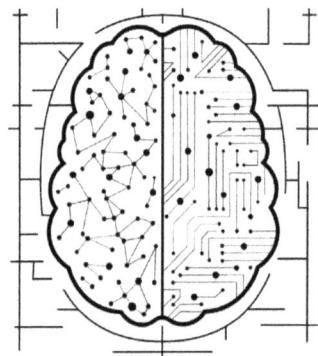

# PART II
# APPLYING THE NOVEL MATRIX

# 8

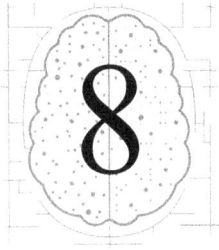

# APPLYING THE
# NOVEL MATRIX

YOUR STORIES HAVE THE POWER to change the world. You can shed light on topics that people would rather ignore, you can prove that impossible things aren't so impossible after all, you can demonstrate what kind of people are good and virtuous.

In order to do that, your story needs a workable vehicle. Your reader has to be able to relate to the story in a way she's learned to understand stories.

Your protagonist is going to do something impossible! Over the course of an amazing story, he will gradually change into a person that can do impossible things. That's why you're telling this story.

Successful stories take the time to build a well-defined universe. Great stories don't leave anything to chance, but establish social rules, physical expectations, and parameters for the supernatural. Amazing authors shape our expectations in advance for how romance works and what technology is available to the characters.

While there are a few exceptions, the three-act structure is by far the most popular storytelling mechanism in modern America. It conforms to our understanding of how people make changes, why we take action, and how we fail and try again. It also prevents the story from becoming too complex to follow. The best stories use the three-act structure to tell a story of agency, in which the character breaks out of what constrains her to take action on her own behalf.

Stories need conflict. Challenges and obstacles aren't good enough, we need mutually exclusive forces at work in opposition to each other. If one thing wins, the other must lose, or it's not a conflict.

We can't reduce our protagonist's world to one magic bullet solution, but we also can't incorporate the infinite complexity of real life. In order to achieve the appropriate complexity for a novel-length work, we identify and focus on five specific conflicts. Three of these conflicts focus on the protagonist's personal journey, while the other two focus on the larger world the protagonist is a part of.

The protagonist won't resolve all of these conflicts. He'll solve some of them, make progress on some of the others, and some will likely remain completely unchanged.

But the protagonist won't do it alone. He's helped by a developed cast of characters. He'll be aided by a guide, a sidekick, a frenemy, and an object of affection. The protagonist will be confronted by an antagonist, who specifically and personally opposes him, and by a mega-antagonist who represents everything that's wrong with the universe.

In Part II, we're going to repeat some of the information from Part I: Understanding the Novel Matrix, but we're going to reframe it to your task of developing a concept for a new novel.

Please take a moment to look through the blank Novel Matrix worksheets in the appendix of this book, or download full-size printable versions at NovelMatrix.com. Part II will provide instructions for filling in these worksheets and planning your next novel project.

DOWNLOAD FULL-SIZE WORKSHEETS

FREE RESOURCES AT NOVELMATRIX.COM

# 9

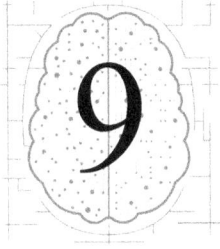

# BUILDING ONE UNIVERSE

ALL GREAT STORIES are set in a universe, and the author must develop that universe on puropse.

The use of the word "universe" here doesn't imply anything of a science fiction sense. Even stories that are set in the "real world" have a developed universe—we just mean a set of expectations that the author develops about the setting of the story.

Romance stories each have their own universe. This is part of what makes *Jerry Maguire, Knocked Up,* and *The Notebook* so different—we have totally different expectations for how the world is supposed to work. All of those stories are set in the real world, right? But oh so different worlds!

It doesn't matter what genre you're intending to work in, every story must have an intentionally developed universe if you want the big moments of the story to hit hard.

The universe of a story includes the social, physical, spiritual, and emotional parameters and expectations for the setting of the story. Our story must answer the questions:

- Where are we?

- What's normal here?

- What is exceptional?

- What is impossible?

A story must establish the rules of the universe, so that later those rules can be broken. If your reader doesn't know what's normal, how will he know when something exceptional has happened?

## YOUR STORY IS NOT SET IN "THE REAL WORLD"

When it comes to your story, there's no longer any such thing as the "real world." What your reader thinks is *real* is entirely subjective to her own experience and expectations.

- Is it normal for a punch in the face to knock someone unconscious?

- Is it normal for people to move in together before they're married?

- Is it normal for a child to shout at his parents?

- Is is normal for people to go to church on Sunday morning?

You could probably immediately answer all of these questions from your own perspective. They're simple enough. But if you surveyed people at random on the street, you would get very different answers to these questions. We may be able to statistically come up with a sort of average position, but on a reader to reader basis, you can't count on any "normal."

It's up to you to educate your reader regarding what's normal in your story.

A reader may show up to the story with a worldview that's very different from yours. If you take the time to teach them what's normal and what's exceptional, they'll accept the story as you tell it. When readers are educated by the author, most of them love stories that are very different from their own experience. If you don't bother to teach the reader, they'll apply their own rules to the universe and likely reject the story.

In *Downton Abbey*, the world experience of the characters on the show is vastly different from our own experience in modern America. We really can't relate to the social ethics that are in place, yet we accept these ethics because the storytellers intentionally established the universe. We feel the characters' pain in their own limitations, even though no one reading this book will likely ever be in any similar situation.

We do know what it feels like to be lonely, misunderstood, or falsely accused. Because we know the rules of the universe, we can empathize on a human level. Without understanding the rules of the universe, we'd feel disconnected and confused.

## FICTION-FED READERS

We also have to consider that for many genres, the reader's "experience" is entirely through other works of fiction. How many readers of action stories have ever actually been in a gunfight? Practically none. Their knowledge of any such thing is based entirely on fictional accounts.

In the TV series *24*, federal agent Jack Bauer will routinely kill six combatants with ten rounds in his pistol. In World War II, it's estimated that about 45,000 rounds of ammunition were expended per enemy soldier killed. In Vietnam, that number is estimated to be closer to 50,000 rounds per kill. Most readers will find Jack Bauer more believable than soldiers that fire nonstop and hit nothing, simply because that's what they've been exposed to. In either case, it's up to you as the author to establish what's normal for your particular story.

The Sam Mendes film *1917* is much closer to "reality." Soldiers run while being shot at in several scenes and aren't hit. Even though we might reasonably argue that this is "realistic," Sam Mendes had to go out of his way to establish this rule before it became important to the story. He included several scenes in which the good guys and bad guys alike fire shots without effect.

For readers of political intrigue, how many of them have ever entertained an ambassador? Brokered a peace deal? Ever even set foot inside of an embassy? Their context is only what they've been fed by other fiction.

Examples abound for virtually any genre. Elves, trolls, zombies, vampires, even cowboys—don't assume the reader has the same definition of these things as you do.

Intentionally establish the rules of your universe. Don't rely on the idea that the reader already knows, or that the rules are "normal." It's up to you to know what the rules are and to demonstrate those rules through story.

## BRINGING THE RULES TO LIFE

Most books don't begin with a list of rules. (Shame on new editions of *Dune* which include a glossary and explanatory appendixes.)

Instead, readers learn the rules of the universe by observing those rules in action.

This is one of the best applications of the old adage, "Show, don't tell." Let the reader experience the rules, and they'll learn them.

You learn new rules every time you enter a new environment. Most of the time those rules aren't explained, you just intuitively pick up on them. So it goes with your reader. As readers, we observe rules in action and we intuitively internalize them.

You can solidify a rule even further by having a character attempt to break the rule and suffer the consequences. What are the stakes? If the stakes for violating a particular rule of the universe are very high, like death or imprisonment, then introduce a disposable character to suffer the punishment.

If talking to the queen receives an immediate death sentence, your narrator could just explain it, or we can watch someone do it and have their head chopped off. Which one will your reader remember more?

When something is especially unique to your universe, it really needs to be established, or there are a lot of rules we need all at once, remember the "stupid guy/smart guy" routine. Have a stupid guy follow around a smart guy, asking "What's that?" "What does this mean?" and "How does this work?" The smart guy can answer all of those questions in dialogue, and it's also a great opportunity for humor and character development.

Your reader will live vicariously through the stupid guy and have all of his questions answered without having to ask.

## PLOT-DRIVEN RULES

Your plot will drive some of the rules of your universe, especially for speculative genres (like fantasy and sci-fi).

Taking the time to establish these rules in advance will ensure the element doesn't feel contrived when it becomes purposeful to the plot.

In *The Matrix*, when Morpheus is captured, the agents try to "hack into" his brain. Through dialogue, the characters back on the ship explain that they can see his brain waves on the monitor, and that the brain waves will change when the hacking is successful. If all of those ideas hadn't been established early on, this would feel exceptionally convenient to the story. But since we've seen monitors with brain waves, and the storytellers have repeatedly reinforced the idea that the human mind is like a computer, the idea doesn't raise any alarms.

In *Star Wars*, Luke doesn't suddenly use "the force" at the end of the movie. While it's the first time Luke uses it to any effect, George Lucas established and reinforced that rule of the universe for two-and-a-half acts before Luke needs it. If we hadn't heard about the force until that moment, it would have been unbelievable.

By *showing* the rules early on, your reader will easily understand and appreciate your plot when those rules become important.

## APPLY THE NOVEL MATRIX

Sometimes elements of the universe are really important to your idea for a story. Maybe everyone has a twin on another planet, love is forbidden between two groups, or medical technology is actually far more advanced than we realize and just kept secret from the public.

Whatever's important, fill that information in first on the Novel Matrix worksheets. The rest you can fill in as you develop your plot, characters, and conflicts. You may end up filling in some elements of the universe at the end.

The worksheet does not include every possible element of the universe, only the most common elements are present. Your story may have other categories of rules that also need to be determined.

As you develop the plot of the story, look for elements that rely on an element of the universe to function. Make a special note of these elements on your universe worksheet, so that you can make sure you're establishing those elements early and maintaining them throughout the book.

It is up to you to define your universe and then intentionally educate your readers by showing them what the rules are.

With a well-defined universe, your story will be more powerful, you'll control the surprise, and you'll establish a diving board for thematic irony.

So many of our favorite stories aren't memorable because of their groundbreaking plot or even the well-developed characters, but because the universe of the story engages and surprises us.

No matter the genre of your next book, so much of your most effective messaging won't come through the plot or the characters, it will come through the universe.

# 10

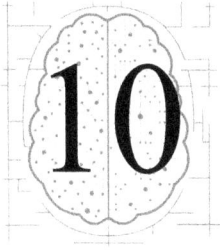

# DEVELOPING THREE ACTS

THIS KEY CANNOT BE OVERSTATED: the hero of the story must do something impossible by the end of the story.

The Impossible Thing doesn't always have to be a grand heroic feat, the Impossible Thing just needs to be something that was impossible for the protagonist to do at the beginning of the story.

If the protagonist is terribly afraid of knives, maybe cooking dinner is a huge accomplishment. If the hero has crippling social anxiety, maybe going on a date is the win. It doesn't matter, as long as the Climax was impossible for the protagonist at the beginning of the story.

Consider these examples:

Jaded dating consultant finds true love. (*Hitch*)

Respectable, soft spoken young man with no interest in crime becomes the most ruthless mob boss in the history of New York City. (*The Godfather*)

Intelligent, ambitious young man with big dreams throws it all away to save his crummy little town from big business, and learns that friends and family are the most important things. (*It's a Wonderful Life*)

Each of these story synopsis are an example of the protagonist doing an Impossible Thing. In these specific examples, the Climax is only impossible because of *who the protagonist is* at the beginning of the story.

The idea that Hitch would date a woman should not surprise us. That's what he's an expert at. Hitch finding true love is only impossible because of who he is as a character, and specifically his traumatic romantic backstory. The character drives the impossibility.

The idea that the son of a mob boss would also become a mob boss is not groundbreaking. But because Mario Puzzo (the author of the book) establishes that Michael Corleone has absolutely no interest in crime or violence, and actually has high ambitions to live a clean life, the idea becomes absurd. The character drives the impossibility.

In most stories, saving the town would be a great impossible feat, but for George Bailey to do it, it requires him to lay down everything that's important to him. He must completely change his paradigm. The character drives the impossibility.

Sometimes the protagonist will do something that's genuinely impossible for anyone. But the only requirement for your story is for the protagonist to do something that's impossible for himself.

In addition to showing the impossible feat at the end, we also have to use the beginning of the story to show why it's impossible.

Your protagonist will do that Impossible Thing over three acts.

This story structure applies to any genre. While we may use terms that are most familiar to action and adventure stories, the concepts are identical for romance, literary fiction, historical fiction, and memoirs.

## REVISITING THE MAJOR PLOT POINTS

In the first act, your protagonist will be destroyed. He'll lose everything that's important to him. He'll go on a 20,000 word journey into the abyss.

Sometimes, he'll literally lose everything, but oftentimes the first act will expose his true priorities.

We all like to think that family is the most important thing, but sometimes losing our money or status would destroy us more than losing our family. How many real life men choose their jobs over their families every single day? As it turns out, they'd rather get divorced than prioritize their families.

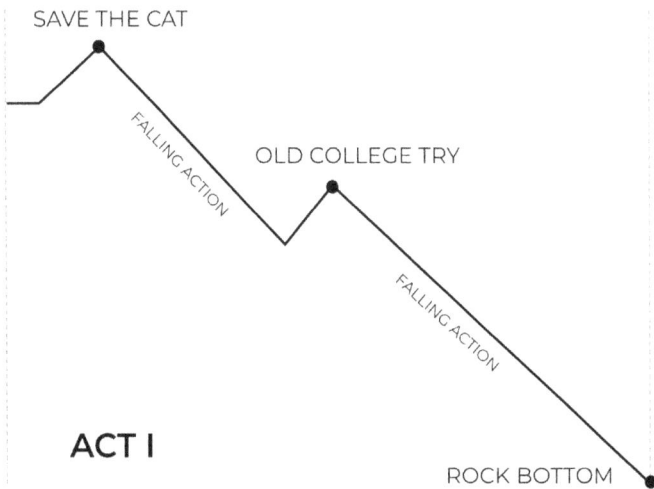

The first act begins with a Save the Cat moment in which the protagonist will do one nice thing. It could be a big deal, like saving a family from a burning car, or it could be a small deal, like smiling at a stranger, returning a shopping cart, or comforting a baby.

Then bad things are going to happen.

The protagonist may be responsible for some of those bad things. He will also likely be the victim of injustice—mistaken identity, misplaced vengeance, natural and man-made disasters, accidents—whatever it takes.

As the protagonist's life spirals out of control, he's going to meet a guide who will offer to set him on a mission. He may accept the mission right away, or he may blow off the guide's counsel.

Either way, the reader will listen to the guide because the guide is wise.

The protagonist will try to escape the bad things that are happening, with no effect.

About halfway through the first act, the protagonist is usually going to make a concerted effort to stop all of the bad things from happening. We call this the Old College Try. He'll push back, but to little effect, as things will continue to get worse.

The antagonist should have a hand in some of the bad things happening to your protagonist, although the antagonist may not yet even know who the protagonist is. The protagonist may just be collateral damage for the antagonist at this point.

Finally, in a definitive moment, the *most important thing* will be torn away from your protagonist. He hits Rock Bottom and he has nothing left to lose. His options are to roll over and die (literally or metaphorically) or to fight back.

Your protagonist is going to fight back. If he doesn't, then you don't have a story worth telling. You just have a really sad short story.

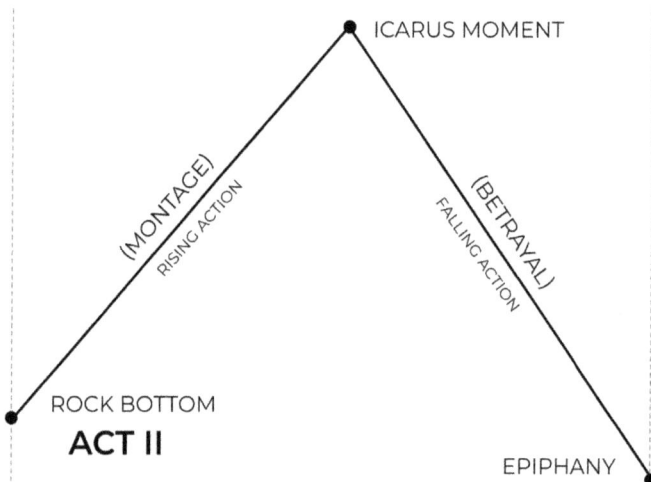

ICARUS MOMENT

(MONTAGE)
RISING ACTION

(BETRAYAL)
FALLING ACTION

ROCK BOTTOM
**ACT II**

EPIPHANY

In the second act, your protagonist is going to attempt to fight the system, but he will fail. By the end of this 20,000 words, your protagonist's life will be more hopeless than ever before.

In most stories, the protagonist will pursue a false goal in the second act. The protagonist is now motivated to take action, but he hasn't learned any lessons or collected the tools, skills, or friends he'll need to really solve the problem. Sometimes he's on the right path but he's just incompetent, other times he's chasing the wrong solution entirely.

The first half of the second act is called the "Montage," because in movies there's often a montage here. (It's a great time to go to the bathroom if you know you can't make it through the whole thing.) Your protagonist is going to do some training, invent a new thing, or collect clues.

This is an upward trending arc in which things feel hopeful after the bruising the protagonist took in the first act.

By the end of this upward arc, all of the story's pieces need to be on the board. All of the major characters need to be introduced prior to the middle of the second act. The reader needs to be subconsciously aware of any tools, skills, or relationships that will be important to the final solution. After the middle of the second act (which should be about halfway through the book), you run the risk of any new introductions feeling contrived (a.k.a. *deus ex machina*). After this point, the protagonist can't suddenly have a new skill.

If the character needs motivation, the object of affection is your tool. The Object is what will draw your character forward into the lion's den. Physically, geographically, or emotionally place the Object in a precarious position in which her destruction is all but guaranteed if your protagonist doesn't do something.

Along this upward arc, your protagonist will make problems for the bad guys. The antagonist and/or mega-antagonist will become specifically aware of the protagonist, and single him out for extreme prejudice.

We call the middle of the second act the Icarus Moment. In a one-two punch, the protagonist will have a great victory coupled with a great catastrophe. Just when things are going really well, everything will get a lot worse.

Usually, but not always, part of this Icarus Moment is that the mega-antagonist has taken or directed some severe, unexpected action against the protagonist and/or his friends.

Through the last half of the second act, things are going to get terrible for the protagonist again—worse than ever before.

Usually what's driving the downward arc of the second act is the antagonist and/or mega-antagonist's attention to the protagonist. If the bad guys weren't aware of the protagonist before, they are now. They are intentionally making the protagonist's life hard and disrupting all of his plans and relationships.

We call the downward arc of the second act the "Betrayal," because often one of your characters will betray the protagonist.

Some good things can happen to the protagonist, but overall, the protagonist's success in his mission trends downward in the latter half of the second act.

The downward arc usually lasts for about 10,000 words. The Epiphany begins the third act.

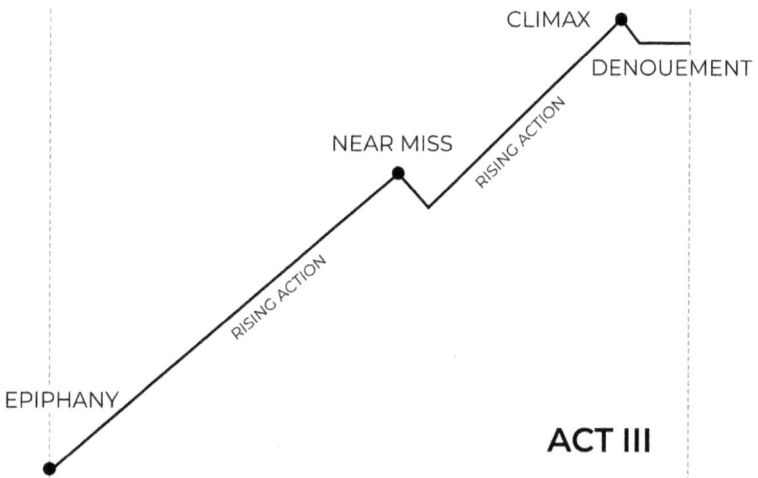

The third act is a mirror image of the first act. Your protagonist is going to learn his lesson, assemble the whole team, and reach victory in the D*riving Conflict* (the conflict that you've identified as the most important).

The third act begins with the Epiphany, in which the big thing will finally come together. This could be a moral lesson that the protagonist has learned, a completion of a tool, skill, or resource, or in the case of a mystery, a discovery or realization that cracks the case.

Your protagonist then applies his epiphany on a generally upward arc through the entire third act.

About two-thirds of the way through the third act, just when things are going so well, the solution will fall apart in the Near Miss. Momentarily, all hope is lost once again.

Oftentimes, if there was a betrayal in the downward slope of the second act, that's reversed to resolve the Near Miss and resume your protagonist's success. If the frenemy walked out in the second act, he'll walk back in just in the nick of time.

However it happens, your protagonist will rally and achieve ultimate success in the Climax.

The story arc relates to the character's seeming success in what the reader understands to be the primary mission. If the character dies, but the mission is achieved (the *Driving Conflict* is resolved), it's still an upward arc.

The Denouement (day-new-mah) follows the Climax. The Denouement should be as short as possible. You've already achieved your big emotional moment in the Climax, the Denouement is your opportunity to quickly tie up any loose ends.

It's important that you don't wrap up every lingering conflict. Most stories will not resolve all five conflicts, and leaving them undone actually makes the story stronger. Your readers will get the big payoff from the Driving Conflict, but still have some loose threads to chew on while they do the dishes.

## FIRST THINGS FIRST

On the three acts worksheet, begin by identifying the big moments in the story:

- Save the Cat

- Old College Try

- Rock Bottom

- Icarus

- Betrayal

- Epiphany

- Near Miss

- Climax

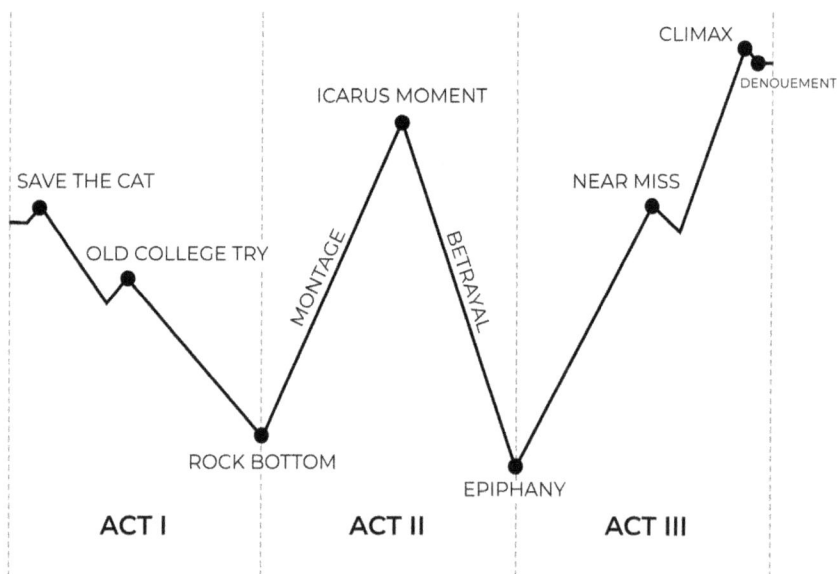

When you do that, chances are that they'll sound ridiculous. How do I get Luke Skywalker from being polite to his aunt and uncle, to his whole family being burned by the empire? Therein lies the beauty of story. You'll fill in the gaps by finding the sequence of events that makes the next Impossible Thing believable.

These vertices should be big, obvious turning points. You want nice sharp edges on your plan—a specific moment where the protagonist's trajectory obviously changes. The hard turns are what will stick in your reader's memory.

Those hard points will tend to naturally round out in the writing as the story becomes complex. If you start with round edges on your plan, then it's only going to get softer. Start with knife-sharp turning points in your plan and you'll end up with comfortable but memorable turns in the story.

After you've identified the major points of the story, then you'll begin to fill in the scenes between.

## KEY QUESTIONS

If you're struggling to plot your story, consider these questions to get your wheels turning:

### Rock Bottom Moment

What would your protagonist say is the worst thing that could happen to him?

What's actually the worst thing that could happen to him?

If the antagonist wasn't targeting the protagonist, what terrible thing might still happen to the protagonist just because of who the antagonist is?

If the protagonist had a really bad day, how would he complete this sentence, "Well at least I still have my _____"? Now have the antagonist, on purpose or by accident, take that thing away.

### Icarus Moment

Before the character has learned a lesson and changed, how would he attempt to fix everything that's gone wrong in his life? On his best day, what would that look like?

What false solution do you want to show in this moment, in order to contrast it to the real solution in the Climax? What message do you want to send about what's true or false—good or bad?

What doesn't the protagonist know yet? What is he still lacking?

What character does the protagonist not yet trust, but he should? What character does the protagonist trust, but he really shouldn't?

How is the protagonist really ruining the bad guy's day, even if it's by accident?

What's the conflict between the protagonist and the antagonist, and what situation would really draw them into direct battle?

## Epiphany

What big revelation would change at least two of the protagonist's conflicts and how he approaches them?

What counsel or good example has the protagonist rejected until now?

Why has the protagonist failed up to this point?

In what way has the protagonist been his own worst enemy up to this point?

What's the fewest number of words someone could say to the protagonist to make him realize the truth?

Is the worst thing in the Rock Bottom moment still the worst thing for the character now? Has he replaced that thing, but in a different way, even if he doesn't realize it yet? Is the protagonist's new *most important thing* better or worse than the one he had at Rock Bottom?

What do you want the reader to learn and apply to her own life?

## IDENTIFYING MINOR PLOT POINTS

Once the major plot has been identified, we'll develop the minor plot points.

Develop the protagonist's primary journey. What needs to happen between your big turning points for it all to make sense and for the Driving Conflict to be resolved?

As you go, you'll choose scenes that develop every other element on your plan, like a web.

All five of your conflicts need to make it to the page, each one needs plot points that develop it.

All of your secondary characters need to be introduced and then maintained. That means that they periodically need to show up in scenes.

You'll begin to fill in minor scenes as they occur to you, and as you complete other parts of the plan. After all, how can you plan to develop all of your conflicts if you don't know what they are yet?

There will be a fair amount of give-and-take in this process. As you identify new elements of the universe, new conflicts, and new characters, you'll come back to your story structure and add more scenes.

Sometimes your plot will inspire other elements of the plan. In order for an important plot point to work in the second act, for instance, you may need a sidekick with a particular skill. You can spring board off of the plot to develop that character, and vice versa.

Work in pencil. You will likely erase elements many times as you make all of the pieces fit together.

The three-act structure is "done" when you've identified all of the major plot points, all of the character introduction points, and most of the minor plot points.

However, even when you finish the story structure, you may not yet have identified every scene that you'll write. That's okay. In a future step, you'll take the concept that you have here and continue to develop and fine-tune it.

## HOW LONG SHOULD THE ACTS BE?

Start by planning acts of equal lengths, of about 20,000 words. Three equal acts of 20,000 words will yield a 60,000 word novel.

However, hold that with a loose hand. It's okay to let the acts shrink and stretch a little bit as necessary.

The most common deviation is to elongate the first act. Especially in speculative genres like science fiction and fantasy, there can be a lot of world-building that has to happen in the first act.

If your genre tends to skew longer than 60,000 words, you can account for that. However, if this is your first novel (or potentially first-to-be-published novel), it is wise to constrain your word count and aim for the shorter side. It is typically inadvisable to write a first novel longer than 100,000 words.

The number of specific scenes or plot points required to reach 20,000 words will deviate greatly from writer to writer. Genre is also a consideration. Fast-paced stories like adventure, thrillers, and many types of romance tend to have short scenes. This gives the reader a sense of velocity moving through the story.

Genres like literary fiction tend to have longer scenes, which allow the reader to feel like they're settling deep into the story.

Look back at other things you've written. Do you see any patterns in the length of scenes in short stories or previous novel drafts?

As you plan the story, it may be helpful to write **one or two** test scenes. Get into your characters a little bit and let them do something, then you'll have a better idea what length of scene blocks you like to write. I know you're probably excited to get started at this point, but don't get carried away and write half of the first act before you've completed your plan. Just write enough to start to feel the story, and then return to your planning. A small writing exercise like this will also be helpful as you develop other sections of the plan.

If you're absolutely unsure how long your scenes will be, start by planning 1,000-1,500 word scenes. This seems to be a comfortable starting point for most beginning writers. At this length, you'll need fifteen-twenty scenes per act.

## INJUSTICE IS YOUR FRIEND

When you're stuck in the plot, consider these strategies for moving things forward.

A good downward story arc will have a balance of bad things that are the protagonist's own fault and bad things that are just plain unfair.

In a downward story arc, injustice keeps things moving forward.

Do something to the protagonist that is absolutely unfair or just plain wrong. The hero's car breaks down, someone spreads a dirty lie, or grandma has a heart attack. Do your worst.

Many novels suffer from a protagonist who is too good—he's too smart, too wise, too capable. In a lot of cases, the author struggles to have the protagonist do anything that the author wouldn't do (with the author's perfect knowledge of the universe and perspective).

Your protagonist needs to make poor choices, keep a secret instead of ask for help, and try things for which he is unqualified. As long as your protagonist is moored by a good Save the Cat moment, he even needs to cross moral boundaries—tell a lie, try to cover an honest mistake, or knowingly pursue a forbidden romantic partner.

In an upward story arc, the object of affection is your tool for keeping the protagonist moving forward. When it seems like the hero could just leave well enough alone and go on with his happy life, the Object pulls him back into the lion's den.

In *Indiana Jones and the Last Crusade*, Indy could rescue his dad and go on home. But his father (the Object) convinces him that he must go back to Berlin to recover the grail diary and stop the Nazis on their quest.

Objects are great at getting themselves into trouble (again), and for some reason the protagonist always falls for the Object's pleas and arguments, even when it's obvious to the reader that it's a terrible idea. Objects make the reader groan, but ultimately the Object will also force the hero into situations that will slingshot him to higher highs.

Injustice, stupidity, and misplaced affection—this is the stuff of real life, and it will keep your plot moving forward.

## DEUS EX MACHINA

*Deus ex machina* kills good stories and it's 100% avoidable.

The phrase literally translates "god from the machine." It's a Latin phrase for a Greek idea.

In ancient Greek dramas, when the story needed to end but it wasn't resolving, an actor would sometimes be lowered down from the sky by a machine. This actor would play one of the various gods, and this god would explain the end of the story and wrap up all of the loose ends. The actor was the "god from the machine."

Super convenient. Problem you can't solve? Plot you can't wrap up? The *deus ex machina* will explain it away for you so the audience can go home.

In modern storytelling, *deus ex machina* is a convenient solution to the plot. We never knew the hero could fly a helicopter, but suddenly she has that skill. Or the hero is losing a fight, and suddenly there's a wrench within reach that he can use to bash the bad guy over the head.

In *The Lord of the Rings*—a treasure trove of *deus ex machina*—just when all seems lost, the army of the dead swoops in at the last moment and easily defeats all of the orcs. From where? Why? Since when? Don't worry about it.

In *War of the Worlds*, all hope is lost when the aliens seem to spontaneously get sick and die.

We prevent *deus ex machina* by establishing the universe early in the story. You may have heard of Chekhov's gun, a famous writing rule that I'll paraphrase, "If you introduce a gun, it must go off."

Let me adapt that and give you Pauquette's rule, "If a gun must go off, make sure the audience knew it was there the whole time."

In application, this means that anything we might need to resolve the story at the end—tools, skills, relationships, natural phenomena—needs to be introduced in the first half of the book.

If a meteor is going to coincidentally fall from the sky and strike the bad guy at just the right time, then the reader needs to see that meteors sometimes fall from the sky and hit people in the first half of the book.

If your protagonist is going to use karate skills to beat up the bad guy at the end, then the reader had better see the protagonist practicing karate in the beginning.

If your hero is going to write an amazing love poem to win the heart of the girl at the end, then the reader must see him at his desk laboring over a sonnet in the first act.

118

It is perfectly reasonable to apply this rule in retrospect. This is one of the great advantages of using the Novel Matrix to plan your work. You may plan or write a scene at the end of the book and realize that your protagonist needs to have a skill or tool to pull it off. That's okay, simply go back to the first act and insert that asset into a scene or create a new scene if necessary.

As you watch and read stories, begin to make note of how great writers plant seeds for the future. What did the protagonist need for the solution at the end of the story? How did the writer cleverly work that element in at the beginning to make you aware of it?

## HOW MANY SENTENCES DOES IT TAKE?

However the plot structure shakes out, you should be able to tell the story in one sentence. It will *always* sound something like this: Character does Impossible Thing.

If you can't tell the story in one sentence, then you can't tell it in 4,000 sentences.

When developing your plot, identify the major turning points first. If you've done it right, each one will seem almost impossible. Then identify the minor plot points that tie those big pieces together and make them possible.

Finally, inject plot points to develop and maintain your secondary characters and all five conflicts.

This is a puzzle. It won't come all at once. Give yourself plenty of time and freedom to ponder, to work out the other elements of your Novel Matrix plan, and then revise, ponder, revise until everything fits just right

The biggest advantage of the Novel Matrix is that it helps you to think through all of these elements now, and to make sure that they work together, rather than writing half a book before discovering a major problem.

As you develop your plan, you'll find problems. That's a win! Any bug you find and fix now would have been a catastrophe 30,000 words from now. You're a hero! You just saved yourself a lot of heartache.

When you find a problem, it's not a mistake. You're an engineer doing research and development. At NASA they try to find and correct all of the problems *before* they strap the astronauts into the shuttle!

By developing your plot in advance, as part of a comprehensive strategy for the story, you will intentionally develop themes and messaging that will resonate deeply with your reader.

Have fun with it and work the plan until it's beautiful.

# 11

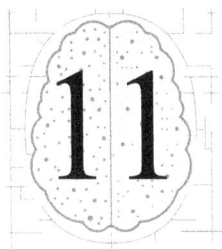

# IDENTIFYING FIVE SPECIFIC CONFLICTS

THE "MAGIC BULLET" fallacy is the idea that there's one solution, a magic bullet, that will fix everything in your life. This is the bread and butter of late night infomercials.

*Buy the Total Gym and you'll get in great shape, find a smokin' hot spouse, and get a better job.*

*Get Axe body spray and women will chase you and your whole life will change.*

I've had the privilege of hanging out with a lot of homeless people in my life, and so many of the people I get to talk to have their own magic bullet. *If I could just get my social security fixed* or *if I could just get to my cousin's house in Georgia...* No matter what the magic bullet is, the sentence always ends about the same, *everything would be different*.

Of course we know that's not true. Most chronically homeless individuals have a myriad of problems that would need to be solved for their lives to change meaningfully.

I can fall victim to magic bullet thinking myself from time to time, and I'm sure you can too. Right now I'm pretty convinced that if I could just finish writing this book, my life would be easier. But life really isn't that simple.

Yet when we write fiction, we often create magic bullets. We create conflicts and problems that are too simple. The stories are shallow and unfulfilling.

And sometimes we do the opposite.

The opposite of the magic bullet is "Aunt Becky." Life is infinitely complex, and Aunt Becky is going to tell you all of it. Aunt Becky is trying to tell you why she had to get her car towed home, but in the process we've rabbit-trailed to why she's thinking about quitting her job, her neighbor Donna's impending divorce, and a story she saw in the newspaper about the government tracking your phone. Two hours later your face hurts from that awkward forced smile and you're pretty sure your neck is going to break in half from nodding like an idiot.

Like Aunt Becky, many novels try to include so much complexity that it's impossible for the reader to follow along. The story becomes bloated and boring.

Conflict is an essential ingredient of storytelling. Remember Donald Miller's definition of story, "A character wants something and they overcome conflict to get it." Without conflict, it's not a story.

Just like the other ingredients, we need the right amount.

If there are too few conflicts, we fall victim to the magic bullet, and the story just feels stretched and contrived. If there are too many conflicts, the novel becomes too dense, difficult to follow, and the reader won't get a satisfying feeling of resolution at the end.

Your challenge is to get the right amount of conflict on the page. Your story needs to exist somewhere between the magic bullet and Aunt Becky.

## WHAT IS A CONFLICT?

A conflict is two things in tension, in such a way that both cannot be satisfied at the same time.

If one thing wins, the other must lose.

Luke Skywalker cannot fulfill his dream of becoming a fighter pilot and maintain his value of being a good nephew. There is no way to do both at the same time. One or the other must fall, or a new compromise must be discovered.

When developing conflicts, it's helpful to state them as two defensible statements—ideas that you could make an argument and present evidence for.

In a literature class, we might state Luke's internal conflict as "Luke versus his identity." That's true to a degree, but it doesn't help us write a story. What about Luke? What about his identity? Well his present identity is the good and helpful son. The identity he aspires to is starfighter pilot.

If we restate the internal conflict as "Luke's family values as a good son" versus "Luke's burning desire to be a starfighter pilot," now we have something to write about. We can now craft scenes that show Luke as a good son, and we can craft other scenes that demonstrate his burning desire to be a pilot. When we put it all together, your reader will "see" the conflict.

The same is true of a philosophical conflict. We might say that *Star Wars* asks the philosophical question, "What is our duty to society?" That's true, but it doesn't give us anything to write about. Instead, we need to identify two philosophical positions that we can present evidence for. We need two specific positions that we can defend until a winner emerges.

In the case of *Star Wars*, "Life is meaningless, get what you can" versus "you must find and fulfill your destiny" are two ideas that we see present in the story. With defensible statements, we can now introduce characters and situations that present and demonstrate each position. It's now something that you can take action on as a writer.

State your conflicts as two specific elements in tension. It will make your writing so much easier.

## YOUR FIVE CONFLICTS

Every great story has five major developed conflicts.

Three of these conflicts relate only to the protagonist (the "Little

World"). Aside from minor fallout, success and failure start and stop with the hero.

The protagonist is also a member of a bigger struggle. Two of our conflicts pit people groups, institutions, and systems against one another (the "Big World").

## LITTLE WORLD CONFLICTS

| INTERNAL | EXTERNAL | PHILOSOPHICAL |
|---|---|---|
| *TWO INCOMPATIBLE THINGS THE PROTAGONIST DESIRES* | *A DIRECT CONTEST WITH A NAMEABLE ENTITY* | *TWO OPPOSING WORLDVIEWS* |

## BIG WORLD CONFLICTS

| INTERNAL | EXTERNAL | PHILOSOPHICAL |
|---|---|---|
| X | *TWO PEOPLE GROUPS IN CONFLICT* | *TWO IDEAS OF HOW THE WORLD OUGHT TO BE* |

# LITTLE WORLD INTERNAL CONFLICT

Your hero has a burning issue that really only takes place in his own head or heart. Most of the time this is most easily stated and developed as two competing desires. These competing desires often have moral implications.

This is a Little World conflict and it revolves around the protagonist's feelings. There may be some fallout or through-play from the resolution of this conflict, but it's not going to change the world.

Remember that the ideas must be mutually exclusive. As the character initially understands them, they can't both be done at the same time. There can't be an obvious compromise.

Usually the character will ultimately have to choose one or the other. However, sometimes the character may find a new way to understand one of those desires and discover a both/and position. For instance, George Bailey in *It's a Wonderful Life* doesn't fully surrender his desire to be successful at the feet of his desire to help his town. Instead, he reframes what "success" means—"No man's a failure who has friends."

Here are some common internal conflicts to get your wheels turning. All of these have been written many times, so you're free to take it right from here and make it your own.

- Character desires to be successful in profession versus character desires to prioritize what's "really important" (family, friends, self-sacrifice)

- Character desires to better his life in a specific way versus character really likes things to stay the same

- Character wants relationship versus character wants to do everything himself

- Character wants to stop the bad guy at any cost versus character wants to maintain his moral integrity

- Character wants to honor family versus character wants to be his own man

Obviously, these are generic, but use them as fodder. There are an infinite number of ways to express and develop these conflicts.

It's important to note that the two statements don't always need to be diametric opposites. Oftentimes more thoughtful stories create a conflict that is nuanced. To return to George Bailey in *It's a Wonderful Life*, being successful and helping your town aren't necessarily opposites. For most people, these ideas could certainly be compatible with each other. There's something about who George is, how he understands his identity and his family history that force these two compatible ideas into tension with each other. George as a character *is* the tension between the ideas.

The internal conflict may or may not resolve. If it's resolved, it's usually because the protagonist definitively chooses one thing over the other. A great writer *shows* this choice.

The internal conflict can also resolve because the character gains a new understanding of himself.

Sometimes, the protagonist finds a way to compromise between the two positions.

APPLICATION: For the Little World Internal Conflict, develop two competing ideas that the protagonist is wrestling with. What are two things that the protagonist wants at the same time?

## LITTLE WORLD EXTERNAL CONFLICT

The Little World external conflict is most easily stated as the protagonist versus the antagonist.

Importantly, the protagonist and antagonist must have mutually exclusive goals. One will win and the other will lose.

Luke Skywalker wants to destroy the Death Star, but Darth Vader would very much like it to stay intact.

It's important to note that the conflict is with the other person, the protagonist's specific objective is secondary to that. The protagonist's objective is just a way to draw these two characters into contest with one another.

Sometimes the external conflict manifests because both characters want the same thing—a job, a romantic partner, a meal, or to be the hero. Only one of them can have it.

In other cases, the protagonist wants to achieve something that the antagonist is determined to prevent.

The external conflict is resolved by destruction or conversion.

With destruction, the protagonist soundly beats the antagonist, who may or may not be literally destroyed.

With conversion, the antagonist ultimately changes his way of thinking and decides to support the protagonist's goals.

Romances are often solved by conversion. In many romance stories, the antagonist is the romantic interest. Through the course of the story something impossible will happen—the antagonist will "fall in love" with the protagonist and the conflict is resolved.

You can frame this external conflict by beginning with your Impossible Thing or beginning with your antagonist, whichever comes easier to you.

If you know the Impossible Thing the protagonist will do, ask yourself, "Who would want the same thing?" Or, "Who would want to stop this from happening?" That's your external conflict.

If you start with a great idea for an antagonist, then ask yourself, "What's something that my antagonist and protagonist would both want?" Or, "What's something that the protagonist might try to achieve that the antagonist absolutely would not be willing to let happen?"

APPLICATION: Identify the Little World External Conflict. How does it relate to the Impossible Thing? Do the protagonist and antagonist both want the same thing, or do they have opposing goals? Will the antagonist be defeated by destruction or conversion?

## LITTLE WORLD PHILOSOPHICAL CONFLICT

The protagonist is trapped between two ways to understand the world.

The Bible has the original philosophical conflict in the garden of Eden. God said, "I'm enough for you." Satan said, "Are you sure you couldn't do more on your own?" Two different characters presented two different ideas, and the story demonstrates plausible arguments for each.

As with all of our conflicts, the Little World philosophical conflict should be presented as two defensible propositions.

We might know as consumers of literature that a book is asking the question, "What's the value of money?" but as a writer, that idea is so abstract as to be useless. Instead, we state the question as two distinct positions. "Money can buy happiness" versus "money is always evil."

With two clear positions, you can craft scenes and characters that support each statement separately. The protagonist is caught between the two worlds and must ultimately choose how he'll view the world.

Two distinct statements will also create a much more nuanced, complex, and emotionally satisfying debate. "What's the value of money?" is very general, and could really be the culmination of several debates, such as:

Money is the root of all evil versus money can't buy love

Money is the root of all evil versus only poor people believe money isn't important

Usually in real life we're not debating polar opposites. For instance, as a culture, racism is a big debate right now, but no reasonable person is putting forth the idea, "Racism is good." The debate is not racism is good versus racism is bad. Instead, we're debating nuanced differences in our understanding of the idea of racism (at least in comparison to the historical race debate).

In the case of our money examples, consider how I can completely change the nature of the conflict just by changing one of the two statements a little bit:

Money is the root of all evil versus only poor people believe money isn't important

Can become:

Money is a means to an end versus only poor people believe money isn't important

We're now telling a different story with a different conflict. Some ninth grade English class might someday reduce it to the same "theme" either way, but the emotional impact of the story is going to be very different.

Sometimes the internal conflict or the external conflict will inspire the philosophical conflict, but it should not just be a restating of something that's already in one of the other boxes. It should stand alone.

For example, if my internal conflict is: "Mark's desire to be rich" versus "Mark's desire to take over the family plumbing company," my philosophical conflict should not be "Money is the measure of happiness" versus "Family is the most important thing."

It's too closely related, I'm just restating the internal conflict, so my novel will feel thin. If I take the concept just one step further to something like, "Financial security for his family is a man's most important duty" versus "Honoring family is more important than financial security," now I'm adding to the conversation. I'm building another layer into the story.

You need to be able to defend, with integrity, both philosophical statements, even if you don't agree with one of them. You might know who the clear winner of the contest is, but you still need to give the other side an honest treatment. Readers can smell a straw man from a mile away (and this is a big reason Christian fiction frequently falls flat).

Articulating a fair argument for both sides will ultimately drive your point home even harder. Too many stories make their opposition look foolish, and it only discredits the work. Is it more impressive if a big man beats up a small man, or if a big man bests another big man? The bigger you allow the opposition to be, the more you'll reinforce the value of the winner.

Most often, the philosophical conflict is represented by two secondary characters. The frenemy and the guide are natural choices for this, especially if there is going to be a clear "right" side in the end.

You could use other characters to carry these viewpoints. Sometimes even the protagonist holds one of the contested viewpoints, though usually only if he'll change his mind by the end of the story.

Not all of your conflicts in the novel will resolve. You could introduce a philosophical conflict to which you don't know the answer and that you are not able to resolve.

APPLICATION: The Little World Philosophical Conflict must present two clear, defensible positions. Identify two positions that the protagonist must contend with. Can you make a reasonable, informed argument for each opinion, even if you disagree with one or both of them? Look to your frenemy and your guide—with what viewpoints might they naturally confront the protagonist?

## BIG WORLD EXTERNAL CONFLICT

Your protagonist has his own stuff going on, but he's also playing a part in a larger story. The Big World is where we see that larger contest play out.

The Big World external conflict is almost always two people groups who are in contest with each other.

These groups can be anything, real or imagined, big or little. Rebels versus Alliance, Republicans versus Democrats, dog people versus cat people.

This is the Big World, so if the protagonist achieved victory in this area, we would see lasting change in the "world."

Most often, your protagonist will initially identify as a member of one of these groups. However, in some stories the protagonist is caught between them and must choose.

As you consider this question, ask yourself, what groups is my protagonist a member of?

What outlandish thing could the protagonist do to achieve lasting systemic change in the universe of my story?

In most stories, one of the people groups will be led by the mega-antagonist, who is just plain evil. So who are the really bad guys in your story? The ones who are just plain evil?

What groups is your antagonist a member of?

In most cases, this big external conflict will not resolve. The protagonist might provide an incremental shift or a minor setback to one group, but it's unlikely (and often unbelievable) that your protagonist would achieve major systemic change in the course of a single novel.

These people groups are going to be represented throughout your story. It may be helpful to think of your Big World external conflict through the lens of "world building" as much as through the lens of plot.

APPLICATION: Identify two major people groups who are in active conflict in your story. These two groups should relate to the protagonist and the Impossible Thing. Is the protagonist a member of one of the groups in the beginning of the story? Will his group membership change by the end?

## BIG WORLD PHILOSOPHICAL CONFLICT

Your story is also going to ask a big question about a big topic. The nature of good and evil. Principles of good governance. Gender relations.

This is often where genre fiction falls shallow. We have to ask a hard question that probably won't tie up nicely with a bow at the end. This is how your story becomes more than just the action and characters on the page.

Just like the Little World philosophical conflict, we need to state this conflict as two positions which you can advocate for in good faith (even if you don't agree with one of them). I mean that. If I want to write a book about slavery, I need to prop up a character who will make a really compelling argument about how it's good for the economy, it's better conditions than the slave's country of origin, etc. The bigger you allow the "bad" viewpoint to be, the more impressive your steamroller will be when the "good guys" win!

Oftentimes, these philosophical statements will relate closely to the people groups in the Big World external conflict. What's a driving idea of each people group?

As with the Little World philosophical conflict, these statements don't need to be direct opposites—they just need to be in contest with each other. It's sometimes more realistic if these aren't polar opposites.

For instance, if I was writing a book about the American Civil War, I could say that the Big World philosophical conflict is "slavery is bad" versus "Slavery is good." However, it might be more authentic, nuanced, and satisfying to the reader to identify the conflicts as "Slavery is an abhorrent evil that must be stopped at any cost" versus "Self-governing states are a foundational principle of our country and must be protected at any cost."

(I'm not trying to make any commentary on the Civil War here. I just want to demonstrate an earnest approach to authentically represent the people groups in a story.)

It's very interesting when two ideas aren't diametric opposites yet still cannot exist in the same space. That gives us a lot more to think about, especially when both ideas are good ideas in their own right but there's some application that makes them incompatible.

The Big World philosophical conflict mostly makes its way to the page through world-building. However, in many stories the protagonist or the guide will become a mouthpiece for the "good" people group and the mega-antagonist will be a mouthpiece for the "bad" people group.

Here are some good questions to ask to start the wheels turning:

- What are the cultures of your people groups? How does this culture dictate how they relate to each other and to outsiders?

- How is propaganda used in these groups?

- What is the mythology of these groups? Even real, modern groups have mythology—a kind of romanticized version of their origin and history.

- What are the stated goals of your big groups? What are unspoken but understood goals?

- What do these groups base their credibility and/or authority upon?

- What good thing does each group believe they're fighting for?

- What bad thing does each group choose to ignore in honor of their greater goal?

Explore these ideas and then allow them to flow through your characters onto the page.

Always be specific in identifying your philosophical conflicts.

Especially in the case of your Big World philosophical conflict, it's going to get watered down and muddied up quite a bit in the process of showing it through your characters and filtering the ideas through their personalities. Make sure you're starting with something razor sharp and rock solid so that it's still recognizable on the other side of the blender.

> APPLICATION: Identify two mutually exclusive ideas that are held in contest by the groups you identified in your Big World external conflict. (You could also begin with the Big World phil-osophical conflict and then design two people groups who will manifest those ideas.) If the ideas aren't opposites, what makes them incompatible within the context of this story? What would the world look like if the "good guys" win? What would the world look like if the "bad guys" win?

## INSIDE-OUT CONFLICTS

Some conflicts have to be drawn out in order to manifest on the page, especially internal conflicts. Something has to happen that *shows* what's happening on the inside of the character.

As an example, if a father is dealing with lack of control over his teenage daughter, how will he express that? What elements could you use to show that internal conflict? Perhaps he takes her car keys, secretly searches her room, or hires a private investigator to follow her around. These are manifestations of that internal conflict that your reader can see and understand, which is way better than broadcasting a bunch of internal dialogue to the page.

This is how your internal and philosophical conflicts result in ac-tion on the page.

In *Iron Man 2*, Tony is struggling with self-reliance. In order to show this, the storytellers give him a problem with his blood toxicity. This is an output of his internal struggle of what he can do himself versus when he needs a team. It's a plot device that allows the thing happening inside of Tony to make it to the outside.

133

As you're developing your plan, you'll need to be creative about how you manifest those conflicts in the story. But the stuff that happens inside must be expressed in a way that your reader can see.

In what practical ways does the internal conflict impact your protagonist's life? What could you contrive to show us a really good example?

What bearing will the philosophical conflict have on how your protagonist attempts to solve his external and internal problems? What shadow does this debate cast?

Even your external conflicts need to be manifested. It's not enough that there's a guy named Luke and a guy named Darth Vader and they don't like each other. They have to be in contest for something—either they both want the same thing or they want opposite things. Get specific. Get absurd even. You have at least 50,000 words to justify it.

## THE DRIVING CONFLICT

After developing five conflicts, we need to choose one that will be our Driving Conflict. This is the conflict that most closely correlates to the Impossible Thing the protagonist is going to accomplish, and this is the conflict that will be solved by the end of the book.

In many ways, this choice will be the single biggest factor in determining what kind of book you're writing.

Any of the five conflicts can be your Driving Conflict, though in most cases a Little World conflict is a better and easier choice.

Once you've chosen your Driving Conflict, put a square around it on your plan.

This conflict you choose should match your Climax. Your Driving Conflict is what will get the most page-time, and it will be the resolution your reader is hungry for. In the Climax, what Impossible Thing is the protagonist going to achieve?

Remember that the protagonist's Impossible Thing is a thing that's impossible *for him at the beginning of the story*. The internal conflict can be your Driving Conflict, as long as you're prepared to *show* a resolution to that conflict.

After you identify the protagonist and the Climax, you should be able to say the story in one sentence. "A [insert description of Protagonist without agency] will [insert Impossible Thing]." Are you satisfied with that sentence? Does it sound like the genre you want to write?

If not, change it. The point of planning is to identify things that are unsatisfactory so that you can change them *before* you start.

If it doesn't sound like the genre you intended, perhaps you're focusing on the wrong conflict. If it doesn't sound like an interesting story, perhaps your Climax isn't impossible enough, or your beginning protagonist isn't weak or trapped enough.

A bad story in one sentence will be an even worse story at 4,000 sentences. Continue working on the plan until you have a riveting one-sentence story.

As a second test, once your three-act structure is roughly laid out, try telling your story in three sentences. Is each part an interesting story?

*Star Wars* might sound something like this.

1. A teenage farm boy who dreams of being a starfighter pilot is invited on a secret mission for a righteous rebellion and initially refuses, but accepts after the bad guys kill his whole family.

2. He receives training from a master of a magical force and saves a princess, but then his mentor is killed and he puts the whole rebellion in danger.

3. He goes to battle in a space ship and uses his new magical powers to defeat the bad guy and blow up the biggest weapon in the universe.

Each of those parts is a great story on its own. I'm intrigued. I want to know how those things are going to work out.

If you have a great one-sentence story, and a great three-sentence story, then you're on the right track for a great 4,000-sentence story.

## CONFLICT AND STAKES

Conflicts are the lifeblood of story. Conflict is closely related to the idea of "stakes."

Stakes are what keep your reader flipping pages.

Stakes are the idea that if the hero fails, something really bad will happen, but if the hero succeeds, something really good will happen. Your reader needs to know what the stakes are—that's why they keep turning the page.

Sometimes we can overemphasize the negative stakes and fail to develop the positive ones. Loss aversion is the statistically proven idea that most humans would rather not lose something than gain the same thing. Given the choice, most people would prefer not to lose $100 over finding $100 on the sidewalk. This is a powerful psychological principle that's often underused in fiction.

John Steinbeck is a master of developing both positive and negative stakes. In *Of Mice and Men*, the potential negative stakes of Lenny's issues are obvious from the beginning. Lenny is a ticking time bomb. However, the story comes alive when Candy agrees to join Lenny and George's vision and the grand positive outcome the men have been imagining becomes possible. With positive stakes, the story takes on more gravity than ever before. Now the men can do worse than going from neutral to bad—they stand to lose a potentially happy ending as well.

Imagine it this way—it's bad to fall into a ten-foot deep hole, right? But what if you fall into a ten-foot deep hole from atop a ten-foot ladder?

*Showing* the potential positive outcomes are like helping your reader up a ladder. *Showing* the potential negative outcomes are like digging a hole in front of the ladder. The bigger the potential drop, the better.

Steinbeck accomplishes the same in *The Pearl*. Kino is placed in a position where he will either gain immeasurable wealth or lose everything. The positive stakes are developed as well as the negative ones.

Your stakes often flow from the Little World conflicts and the Big World conflicts working together. As *Star Wars* develops, we begin to believe that Luke overcoming his inner conflict and becoming a starfighter pilot really might have a bigger impact than we could have imagined. The resolution of Luke's Little World just might save the Big World from oppression and tyranny.

## TO THE REST OF THE BOARD

As we identify our story's conflicts, then we look for opportunities to draw those conflicts into focus in our plot.

For instance, if we know that Luke and Darth Vader need to be in conflict, we can fabricate an incompatible goal. Luke wants the Death Star destroyed, Vader wants it protected. Now that conflict has to come to a head. They can no longer be enemies at a distance. The conflict must resolve one way or the other. They can't both have what they want. Luke will make efforts to destroy the Death Star. Darth Vader will take action to protect it.

The guide will send Luke down the path. If we need any help, the object of affection will give Luke a push whenever necessary.

The internal conflicts must manifest themselves on the page. Luke wants to be a starfighter pilot, so he whines to his uncle who tells him no. Tony Stark wants to do everything himself, but he has a disease that he can't cure alone.

The philosophical conflicts need vehicles to bring them to the page. Who will advocate for those opposing ideas? What situations will make the difference in those ideas obvious?

All five conflicts must be developed and represented in scenes in the plot. While some of the conflicts will get more emphasis than others, they all must be present.

Most writers tend to focus on too few conflicts. Romance, literary fiction, and adventure are all prone to this kind of thin development. Oftentimes the story will rely on only one or two major conflicts, and then there's a bunch of loose threads that never get developed.

Some writers, especially in genres with complex world development like high fantasy and political thrillers, tend to spread their net too wide and develop more than one Driving Conflict. The end is like a middle school band concert where no one's really sure when to start clapping.

Memoirists, take special note. This is where you're most likely to run into trouble. You're writing a story about your whole life, and your life is legitimately infinitely complex. But you can't include all of that. Force yourself to identify five specific conflicts that you're going to write about, and then don't wander off.

Regardless of your genre, your book can't be about everything. Identify five specific things that you're going to consistently return to. Force yourself to continually live inside of that box. With that in mind, you're going to write a great story that your audience will understand, relate to, and adore.

We'll discuss subplots in Chapter 13. Subplots happen in addition to your five primary conflicts, but they should hang off the plot like ornaments hang from a Christmas tree. Subplots operate with different expectations than the five primary conflicts you'll identify for your story.

Conflicts give you a lot to think about! You probably won't fill out all five boxes off the top of your head. You'll need to carefully consider what you want to talk about, who your characters are, and the big points of your plot. And that's the fun of it!

Enjoy the concept-level thinking you get to do here. Get your hands dirty. Think it through and make it great, then make it even better. Knowing your five conflicts will pay off in big ways as you dig into the writing of your novel.

The magic bullet is a lie. Aunt Becky is a terrible storyteller. Five conflicts is the magic number that will make your story just right. If you develop all five conflicts, your story is practically guaranteed to cultivate compelling themes!

# 12

# A DEFINED CAST OF CHARACTERS

YOU DON'T NEED to fill out the Novel Matrix in order. There's a fair amount of bouncing around to do. But if you did do it in the order I've described here, you probably already know a lot about your characters just from the plot and conflicts.

Your story needs a protagonist, four helpers, and two bad guys. You have a duty to maintain all of these characters—your reader expects to know how they turn out.

We do see a fair amount of variation in the number of characters. The important thing is that you incorporate every function listed here into your story.

When a character function is missing, your reader can feel it.

Let's revisit the character archetypes and explore some best practices for each one.

## PROTAGONIST

Every story needs a hero.

Even if your genre doesn't have a typical "hero," we still need someone who is going to accomplish something impossible. Even if it's only impossible for the character, that still makes him heroic.

Writing a novel is impossible. When you finish it, you'll be a hero too.

Protagonist—our first champion.

Your Protagonist is usually the only character who will change over the course of the novel—I mean real, heart-level change. Your other characters might shift a little bit, but your protagonist is going to transform into something new, like a butterfly emerging from its chrysalis. (If your antagonist is defeated by conversion, he'll change, too.)

One of my favorite things to do with excellent novels is to read the last chapter and then the first chapter, just to see how different the protagonist is. If the author has done her job, the changes are catastrophic. Over the course of the novel, this was a gradual and well-justified change, and the reader didn't even consciously know it was happening, but the character is practically a different person.

Of course you have a duty to maintain the protagonist. Your reader is expecting constant updates on his whereabouts and welfare. When the book ends, your reader ought to know the fate of the protagonist with precision.

You also have a strong responsibility to develop the backstory of the protagonist. This doesn't mean that you need to have flashbacks or pages of development, but it does mean that if your character can fly a plane, the audience wants to know how he knows that. If he's an expert marksman, the audience wants to know why. If he's a victim of past trauma, the audience expects you to reveal his deepest, darkest secrets.

Even likable protagonists must make decisions which motivate the plot, usually by crossing a moral boundary. Oftentimes we imagine our protagonists as a perfect version of ourselves or as model citizens, just because they're heroes, but this won't drive a novel. Protagonists have to make mistakes, both practical and moral, and get themselves in more trouble.

For example, a protagonist needs to tell a justifiable lie that grows and grows. Perhaps the protagonist needs to disobey his parents and remove a restraining bolt from an R2D2 unit. In romance, the protagonist has to cheat, choose the job over love, or pretend to be someone she's not, in order to spend the whole book overcoming that mistake.

Here's a secret: people like people. Especially when we take the time to get to know them.

Your protagonist can be anyone. If you make the protagonist real and give us a halfway decent Save the Cat moment, your reader will fall in love with the hero—even if she's a terrible person.

## GUIDE

The guide *trope* is a wise old man. You can use that, it's a proven winner, but your guide can be anyone, as long as there's a sense that he's taken the protagonist's journey before.

What must be true about the guide is that the guide must be trustworthy and the guide must say only true things.

The guide is more loyal to the cause (usually of one of the people groups in the Big World external conflict) than he is to the protagonist. We trust the guide to tell the truth, not to keep the protagonist safe. In his loyalty to the higher cause, the guide may send the protagonist on an impossible mission. (Good thing our protagonist is up for impossible things, am I right?)

The guide may be a relay character. If (and only if) the guide is completely removed, a new guide may step into the story. However, if the guide should die or become otherwise incapacitated, there are tons of creative ways to keep his words and persona in the story, even into the third act.

FUNCTION: The guide helps the reader understand the universe and the protagonist's mission.

INTRODUCTION: The reader usually meets the guide early in the first act. The guide is critical to helping the reader understand the universe and also understand the protagonist's goals. It makes sense to deliver those assets to the reader as soon as possible.
APPLICATION: The guide is usually someone who has walked

the protagonist's path before her. The guide is loyal to the cause and must say true things.

The guide is often one voice of the Little World philosophical conflict.

Commonly, the guide dies in the first half of the story. This isn't necessary, but it does force the protagonist into a do-or-die moment. The protagonist can no longer lean on the guide and must step into the mission on her own.

If the guide is completely removed, we may use another character to step into the role. However, more commonly, we see the guide's influence return to the story in creative ways—the protagonist may recall the guide's counsel or have a dream or supernatural experience.

BRAINSTORMING QUESTIONS:
- Who has walked the protagonist's path before?
- Who can represent everything that's good about the "good guys" in the Big World external conflict?
- Who could the protagonist trust, but only reluctantly so?
- Is there a character who could influence the protagonist from *beyond the grave*, literally or metaphorically?
- Is there a character with a secret connection to the protagonist? Or a character who is trusted by someone that the protagonist would trust?

Note that character does not need to *satisfy* all of the listed questions. These are just creative fodder to get your wheels turning if you feel stuck. Some of the questions may not apply to your character or the story you're telling. This note applies to all of the "Brainstorming Questions" throughout this chapter.

# SIDEKICK

The sidekick is unquestionably loyal to the protagonist.

The sidekick serves the function of bringing practical tools and skills to the protagonist without having to justify why he has/knows them.

The sidekick also demonstrates that the protagonist is likable and ought to be helped, while giving the protagonist a sounding board so that his thoughts can get out of his own head and onto the page.

A sidekick can be killed. But be aware that if you take out the sidekick, you're also potentially taking out the protagonist's convenient access to all the things he'll need.

FUNCTION: Bring skills, tools, and resources to the protagonist. Demonstrate likability and be a conversation partner for protagonist.

INTRODUCTION: Almost always early in the first act. Definitely prior to the Rock Bottom moment.

APPLICATION: The sidekick can make reasonable mistakes, but we must never question that he's doing his best to help the protagonist. The sidekick brings stability to the story and gives the reader at least one touch point that she can trust.

Unlike the protagonist, the sidekick can just know things. He can deliver skills, tools, relationships, and resources that the protagonist needs, with little obligation to explain why or how the sidekick has them.

BRAINSTORMING QUESTIONS:
- What help does the protagonist need? What skills, tools, resources, and relationships will the protagonist need to do the Impossible Thing? What kind of character would be a good or ironic candidate to provide those things?
- Why would a character be motivated to be 100% loyal to the protagonist?

- Is there a character who is now in the same place (socially, geographically) as the protagonist, but who comes from a completely different background?
- Other than romantic interest, what kind of character might absolutely adore your protagonist?

## FRENEMY

Your frenemy makes scenes interesting and unpredictable. When the frenemy comes on the page, your reader doesn't know if he might hurt or help your protagonist.

Most frenemies are negative. They have a fantastic capacity to be helpful, if only they'll say "yes" to the cause. A negative frenemy could help, but he won't because he's not yet loyal.

Many times, the negative frenemy will choose loyalty in the third act and this will be a key component of the protagonist's success in the Climax.

A frenemy may also be positive. A positive frenemy is loyal to the protagonist to a fault. Unlike the sidekick, a positive frenemy contributes no useful skills and, despite his good intentions, tends to make the situation worse. But he will pull through and be genuinely helpful at just the right time.

FUNCTION: Introduce a variable to the scene.

INTRODUCTION: In the first half of the book, prior to the Icarus Moment.

APPLICATION: Oftentimes, the frenemy will be a big part of the Betrayal in the downward spiral of the second act. However, in that case, the frenemy is often the deal maker in the Climax, boosting the protagonist to ultimate success.

The frenemy is oftentimes one voice in the Little World philosophical conflict, bringing a new perspective into the protagonist's life.

BRAINSTORMING QUESTIONS:
- Is there a character who has grown up in a similar way as your protagonist, but somehow arrived at a totally different worldview?
- What kind of skill, relationship, or resource is absolutely critical to your protagonist's success? Is there a character who could have access to this asset, and intermittently provide or withhold it?
- What kind of philosophical idea would really challenge the way your protagonist understands the world? (Or for young characters, the way the protagonist was raised.)
- What kind of philosophical idea would be tempting to your protagonist, even if he knows at face value that it's wrong?
- What kind of character would your protagonist find super fun to hang out with sometimes, but at other times find absolutely annoying or even detestable?
- What about your frenemy would your protagonist decide to put up with in order to gain the assets? When would this cross the line and become abusive or manipulative (by either party)?

## OBJECT OF AFFECTION

Your object of affection will practically always make the protagonist's life worse. Ultimately this may lead your protagonist to achieve even greater things, but nonetheless, the Object is nothing but trouble.

Your Object could be a romantic interest, a family relation, or a helpless victim, but it must be someone to whom the protagonist feels an irrational sense of obligation. This obligation could be based on romantic attraction, social order, family responsibility, or a rash vow. It doesn't matter why, but for some reason when the Object gets into trouble, the protagonist responds. If the Object says something is important, the protagonist will say "yes."

Your Object usually will not contribute meaningfully to the protagonist's success. The Object is dead weight—just absolute baggage.

FUNCTION: Pull the protagonist into unnecessary risk and drive the plot forward.

INTRODUCTION: Typically early in the first act, as this may motivate some of the protagonist's initial actions which propel him to his Rock Bottom moment. The Object may be introduced later, but must be present before the Icarus Moment.

APPLICATION: The Object propels the protagonist to action. When the protagonist could realistically pull back from the action or circumvent conflict, the Object will thrust him right back into the middle of the chaos.

Use the Object to accelerate conflict and to draw out the protagonist's Little World internal conflict.

The object of affection often is a romantic interest for the protagonist. It doesn't have to be cliché, that's just real life— love (or sexual attraction) is historically a good motivator.

BRAINSTORMING QUESTIONS:
- To whom does the protagonist have an irrational loyalty?
- What typically drives the protagonist to be uncommonly helpful? Social obligation, romantic attraction, sense of duty, hero complex, moral imperative?
- What kind of person would light the protagonist's Little World internal conflict on fire?
- In what ways does the Object deserve the Protagonist's help and affection?
- What will happen to the Object if the protagonist does nothing?

## ANTAGONIST

Before you object and say that the protagonist is his own worst enemy, let me assure you that we are all always our own worst enemy. This is practically the definition of an internal conflict, and your story *must* have it.

But even if the focus of your story is internal, you must still include real bad guys on the page.

Sometimes the antagonist is just plain bad—some kind of sociopath, psychopath, or narcissist. In modern stories, the antagonist is more commonly a victim of the system to which he is loyal.

It's been a trend in storytelling over the past thirty years to move away from real bad guys and make everyone a victim. Even Jim Carrey's portrayal of *How the Grinch Stole Christmas* gave the Grinch a troubled backstory in which he is just acting out of his own trauma.

Oftentimes we choose the troubled history antagonist because it feels more fair and realistic. Ironically, it's statistically less realistic. Perhaps this is a result of fiction-fed writers.

Bad guys can just be bad guys. According to Dr. Stanton Samenow, a psychologist upon whose work the FBI bases many of their psychological profiling procedures, there is no statistical link between trauma, drug and alcohol abuse, or any other factors we typically assume lead to violent criminal behavior. The "psychosocial" theory of criminal behavior is based on a myth.

According to Dr. Samenow, who worked with hundreds of criminals to formulate his research, bad guys simply choose to commit crimes. The only common factor Dr. Samenow found is the elevation of one's self over the needs of others. Criminals simply justify that what they want is more important than the wellbeing of others, and so they choose to gratify themselves.

That's the only common link. Not trauma, not abuse, not education—they're just self-centered.

A psychosocial theory of deviant behavior which stipulates that bad behavior is a result of trauma may make us feel better, but it wasn't useful to the FBI. It didn't help them catch bad guys. In fact, it caused them to sometimes overlook the bad guy.

It's okay for your bad guys to just be self-centered and sinful. They don't all have to have an abnormally traumatic past. There doesn't have to be a reason that they're bad.

Clive Cussler, one of the bestselling authors of the 20th century proves this. In most of his books, the bad guys are just bad—for no good reason.

For whatever reason you choose, the antagonist will directly oppose the stated mission of the protagonist.

Notably, the antagonist typically believes that his actions are good and justified. In some perverted way, the antagonist sees himself as the good guy in his own story.

Consider Thanos in *Avengers: Endgame*. Thanos destroys half of all life in the universe, but he feels that he's serving the greater good—he's certain that he's doing the hard but necessary thing that nobody else is willing to do. Thanos believes he's the hero.

If you feel like there are lots of bad guys in your story, that's okay, but you must choose one that will really take the lead and represent the group. In *The Hunger Games*, Katniss faces twenty-three other recruits in a showdown to the death, but Suzanne Collins masterfully focuses on Cato as a representative of the group. As Cato goes, so go all the tributes.

The antagonist can be defeated by destruction or by conversion—he can be thoroughly defeated or he can change his position to support the protagonist.

Romance stories often feature a romantic interest who begins as an antagonist, but ultimately converts to "fall in love" with the protagonist.

FUNCTION: Directly oppose the mission of the protagonist.

INTRODUCTION: Usually very early in the first act.

APPLICATION: While the reader typically meets the antagonist very early in the story, the antagonist sometimes doesn't identify the protagonist for special mistreatment right away. In many stories, when the protagonist begins to push back after the Rock Bottom moment, he attracts the special attention of the antagonist for the first time.

148

If the antagonist is defeated by conversion—turning from his errant ways—he may even aid the protagonist in achieving the Climax.

Aside from the protagonist, the antagonist is the only other character who may be dynamic. In the event that the antagonist is defeated by conversion, he will dramatically change as a character.

BRAINSTORMING QUESTIONS:
- What's the protagonist's Impossible Thing? Is there a character who would give his life to prevent that, or who would give his life to achieve the same thing first?
- What kind of antagonist would draw your protagonist's Little World internal conflict most sharply into focus?
- Why does the antagonist believe his actions are justifiable—or even good and reasonable?
- The antagonist must be a real person, but does he represent an idea or a group? How could you use your antagonist to expose your reader to something important?

# MEGA-ANTAGONIST

Your mega-antagonist is the really bad guy who controls the whole system—the Emperor (*Star Wars*), President Snow (*The Hunger Games*), or Mr. Potter (*It's a Wonderful Life*).

Defeating the mega-antagonist (MA) would result in lasting change in the universe of the story.

While the regular antagonist is oftentimes a victim of the system, the MA is almost always just plain evil—rotten to the core.

The MA must be identified in the story, but his level of involvement in the story fluctuates. In stories like *It's a Wonderful Life*, the MA is intimately involved in the plot. In other stories, we may never see the MA "do" much of anything.

The MA is not typically defeated in a single book. In most stories, the antagonist is soundly defeated, but that simply suspends or sets back the MA.

If the MA is defeated, it's usually not realistic for him to be converted. He's too evil for that—the motivations just wouldn't add up. Usually, the MA must be destroyed.

Even in stories that might not lend themselves well to a "super bad guy," there must still be an identified character that represents everything that's wrong with the world. Your reader will understand the fate of the story's universe through the fate of the MA.

If you're having trouble identifying a mega-antagonist, think about the people group that opposes the protagonist in the Big World external conflict. Create a character to be the head of the snake.

FUNCTION: Put a face on evil and represent everything that's wrong with the system.

INTRODUCTION: Prior to the Icarus Moment.

APPLICATION: Oftentimes the MA will first have major influence at the Icarus Moment, and this will be a big factor in the protagonist's downward story arc in the second act.

Prior to the Icarus Moment, the protagonist may not have done enough to warrant the MA's specific attention.

BRAINSTORMING QUESTIONS:
- What sort of person would lead or represent the "bad guys" in the Big World external conflict?
- Is the MA's system necessary in any way, even though it's bad?
- What would happen if the MA had a heart attack today? How would the system change? Would someone else step into his role?
- What does the MA have to offer the protagonist? Could the protagonist ever be enticed to convert?
- What type of evil does the MA embody? With that in mind, what can you use the MA to teach the reader?

150

## TERTIARY CHARACTERS

Your story will have many other characters, and in most cases, there's really no need to plan and develop them ahead of time. You can simply create them as the scene requires.

Need a cab driver, bartender, hotel clerk, or evil henchman? Throw them in. Have fun with it.

It's actually important that we *don't* develop these characters. Your reader can really only care about so many people, you can't bog every character down with an elaborate backstory and expect the reader to fall in love with everyone who graces the page.

Develop the seven identified character types, but your tertiary characters simply exist for a minute and then disappear.

Just let these characters be perfunctory—let them perform their function and get out of the way.

A classic mistake is to spend too much time developing henchman. Your reader can only keep track of so many characters, and your antagonist and MA are the characters who really carry weight. Over developing henchman will usually only confuse your reader and bog down the story. There are some exceptions, like political thrillers, in which there may be a more elaborate ecosystem of bad guys, but nonetheless, exercise caution and generally rein in the development of all of the bad guys.

Just like any tertiary character, let the henchman perform their function, have some fun with them, and then get them out of the way—gone as quickly as they came.

Your story can use as many tertiary characters as it needs. However, if a function can be performed by one of our six secondary characters and there's no good reason not to, then use the secondary character. Don't let your tertiary characters steal opportunities for the secondary characters (the characters we really know and love) to play and develop.

## COMBINING CHARACTERS

Many stories combine character types for fun results, you may too. The important thing is to make sure that the functions are represented. For this reason, some character types cannot be combined. For instance, a character could not be both the sidekick and the frenemy. The function of the sidekick is to be loyal to a fault and always help the protagonist, while the function of the frenemy is to only sometimes help.

| | GUIDE | SIDEKICK | FRENEMY | OBJECT | ANTAGONIST | MEGA-A |
|---|---|---|---|---|---|---|
| GUIDE | | | ✓ | ✓ | | |
| SIDEKICK | | | | | | |
| FRENEMY | ✓ | | | | | |
| OBJECT | ✓ | | | | ✓ | |
| ANTAGONIST | | | | ✓ | | |
| MEGA-A | | | | | | |

**LIKELY CHARACTER COMBOS**

The guide can be your frenemy, because he's loyal to the cause, not the protagonist. In a properly crafted story, you could make it work.

You may also combine positive and negative characters. Your antagonist can be the object of affection. This is often a feature of romance and makes a great twist in adventure stories.

Your reader can't name these character archetypes, but she does know them. Combining them is a way to surprise your readers without upending them.

## REASONABLE DEVIATIONS

The plot structure and the five conflicts are rock solid. Don't mess with a good thing, just use the tools that work.

Characters have a little bit more flexibility. The functions listed

## COMPLETE CHARACTER FUNCTIONS

| ARCHETYPE | FUNCTION |
|---|---|
| GUIDE | 1. EXPLAINS THE UNIVERSE<br>2. ESTABLISHES THE PROTAGONIST'S MISSION |
| SIDEKICK | 1. PROVIDES TOOLS, SKILLS, AND RESOURCES<br>2. ESTABLISHES LIKEABILITY |
| FRENEMY | 1. INJECTS A VARIABLE INTO THE SCENE<br>2. MAY BE POS. OR NEG. |
| OBJECT OF AFFECTION | 1. CATALYZES THE PROTAGONIST TO ACTION<br>2. IS NEVER HELPFUL |
| ANTAGONIST | 1. DIRECTLY OPPOSES PROTAGONIST<br>2. OFTEN A VICTIM OF THE SYSTEM |
| MEGA-ANTAGONIST | 1. REPRESENTS EVERYTHING WRONG WITH THE UNIVERSE<br>2. JUST PLAIN EVIL |

here are important. For instance, you need a character that will make your protagonist do irrational things. You also need a character that is unpredictable. But as long as those functions are present and available to your plot, you can get creative.

We've already discussed character combinations, but you could give each functional character a tag-along buddy, like *Star Wars* does. C3PO has no real plot function, he's just comic relief and does whatever R2D2 does. The same is true of Chewbacca, he's only a shadow and extension of Han Solo.

One of the biggest mistakes you can make is to try to write a story without bad guys. Remember that a conflict is two things in tension. It's nearly impossible to develop real conflict without real people to oppose the protagonist.

Have fun with the characters. Take the time to develop them, but also give the characters space to become themselves on the page.

# 13

# WHAT ABOUT SUBPLOTS?

SUBPLOTS BRING LIFE to your characters. A subplot is a secondary story happening within the framework of your protagonist's main story. Subplots bring depth and complexity to your characters.

*Approach subplots as character development.* Your subplots aren't going to drive the story, they're not going to provide a sense of satisfaction or catharsis for your reader. That's not their purpose.

As such, subplots typically don't need to be overplanned. Minor subplots have a tendency to pop up as you go. Naturally as you write, you'll piece in backstory, romantic tension will flare up and evaporate, and your secondary characters will get distracted by shiny things. Have fun with those things, just don't chase them. Let them spring up and let them die.

You should, however, plan three to five subplots you intend to intentionally develop in the story. Just like your secondary characters, when you develop a subplot and reference it multiple times, you have a duty to maintain that subplot through the rest of the story. Your reader will want to know what happened.

These developed subplots usually tie into the primary plot in some

155

way, but they do not have to.

There are two primary sources for these subplots: side interests and secondary character plots.

## SIDE INTERESTS

Side interests are plots that revolve around the protagonist, but are secondary to the main plot of the story. As an easy example, in most genres, the protagonist will have a romantic interest. It may be cliché, it may be corny, but readers respond to it.

This romantic subplot will often have virtually no relationship to the main plot whatsoever, but if there are a man and a woman among our primary and secondary characters, you can be pretty sure they'll fall in love and kiss before the story's over.

In *The Godfather*, Michael Corleone is primarily concerned with his crime family's business, but he's also trying to fall in love and have a regular family.

In *Iron Man 2*, Tony Stark's main interest is stopping the big bad Russian criminal. However, he's also coming to terms with giving control of his company to Pepper Potts.

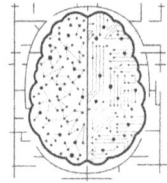

A romantic interest is a very common example, but side interests can come in all kinds of flavors. What else does your protagonist want? Don't go overboard, it should only be one or maybe two things, and it's not going to get a lot of spotlight. But pulling in a competing side interest will complexify the hero's motivations just a little bit.

This is also a great question to ask about your antagonist. What does he wish he was doing right now instead of having to put the stomp on your good guy?

A great place to look for side interests is to ask, "If my protagonist didn't have to be doing this, what would she be doing instead? Where does she wish she was?"

Keep the side interests very simple, they should not materially compete with our five identified conflicts. The side interests are not what the audience came for, they're just bringing complexity to the character.

## SECONDARY CHARACTER PLOTS

Your secondary characters are each the protagonist of their own stories.

It's important that we don't overplay secondary character sub-plots. Your reader has no expectation that these secondary character plots will resolve within the framework of the primary story you're telling, and resolving all the secondary character plots will feel hokey.

Subplots are the lettuce that you put under the deli meat cuts on the tray. Nobody's planning on eating the lettuce, it's just there to make the rest of the stuff look pretty.

It's important that your protagonist (and maybe your antagonist) is the only character that changes significantly within the framework of the story. Your protagonist will become a better person, but every-one else will basically stay the same. It would be very difficult to fully resolve a subplot without making the secondary character dynamic, which would draw emphasis away from your protagonist.

In *Star Wars*, Han Solo is trying to pay back Jabba the Hut for an outstanding debt. This is a secondary character plot. It brings com-plexity and realism to Han Solo's character. It's often a motivating factor for the decisions he makes. Yet he does not resolve this plot. (The storytellers utilize the plot in the second movie to move Han Solo to the position of object of affection.) No one left *Star Wars* feeling shortchanged because they didn't know how the Jabba the Hut thing worked out for Han. It doesn't matter.

Princess Leia is trying to maintain diplomatic relationships across the galaxy. This brings complexity and realism to her character, and is a consistent motivating factor for her, but she makes no progress on this plot in the course of the story.

*Home Alone* is a great example of obvious subplots. Kevin Mc-Callister, who has been left home alone and must protect his house from robbers, has his own subplots—side interests of learning to run a household and a quest to have Santa somehow return his family.

The secondary characters are rife with subplots. Kevin's mother, Kate McCallister, has a subplot in which she'll do anything to get home to her son, which has both an external component (the challenge of getting home from France the day before Christmas) and an internal component (her guilt of forgetting him in the first place). Yet she undergoes no change and learns no major lessons in the course of it.

In this example, the subplot does resolve and Kate is successful. As a children's Christmas movie, the storytellers exploit an intentional feeling of synchronicity and we expect an unrealistically happy outcome.

However, in most cases, secondary character plots almost never resolve, they simply bring complexity to the characters. They're not spotlight features and we shouldn't give them too much page time, but they will bring life and depth to the characters.

Many secondary character plots can be developed with carefully placed lines of dialogue within existing scenes.

## SUBPLOTS IN ACTION

Most novel length stories include three to five developed subplots. There can be more, after all, every character is theoretically a protagonist of his or her own story. As you develop creative ways to motivate your characters, they probably each have threats, dreams, and backstory. But nonetheless, a reader can only give serious attention to a limited number of them. Three to five is typically the right number to develop and maintain.

Even in complex storytelling, the subplots are intentionally restrained. In *The Departed,* as an example, we focus on three major characters, but with the exception of Billy Costigan (Leonardo DiCaprio), the subplots are extremely limited and the characters themselves are relatively one-dimensional. Frank Costello (Jack Nicholson) has no subplots of note, and Colin Sullivan (Matt Damon) has only a romantic entanglement subplot. When you add it all up, we're still in that three to five subplots range.

To develop subplots, first look at your protagonist for side interests. Does he have other compelling goals that dovetail with the primary plot? Your protagonist probably has lots of interests, but typically your subplots should have some relationship to the main course of events so that they can naturally intersect. For instance, if your protagonist is going to have a romantic interest, in most cases it makes sense for it be with one of the six secondary characters, not another random person that we'll have to totally step outside of the story to visit.

Is there a particular side interest that reinforces the Little World internal conflict and will *show* another facet of that conflict?

The protagonist's romantic interest is a very typical subplot. It may feel overdone, but readers almost always like it, regardless of the genre. Does it make sense for your protagonist to be romantically interested in one of the secondary characters? Her interest can even be in the antagonist.

What other interests intersect with the plot? As your character changes in order to become a better person and accomplish her mission, what else will need to change?

- In *Home Alone*, Kevin has to figure out how to do laundry and get food—it's a natural output of the story.

- In *Star Wars*, Luke Skywalker has to learn to use the force—it's really ancillary to the Driving Conflict, but it bears a direct relationship to the action of the story.

- In *Raiders of the Lost Ark*, Indy has to overcome his bad blood with a former romantic fling in order to assemble the tools he needs.

In each of these cases, the subplot is truly secondary. You could remove it without changing the plot, the story would just lose some complexity. But in all three cases, the subplot bears a direct relationship to the plot. From a practical perspective, that makes it easy to work in. The storytellers crafted in scenes specifically to service these subplots, but the reader never feels like, "Why are we talking about this?" These subplots naturally intersect with the main plot.

Next, look at your secondary characters. They're each the protagonist of their own story. Are any of those stories particularly compelling or do they bear a relationship to the Driving Conflict?

Your frenemy and object of affection are typically your best candidates. These characters have the capacity to operate far outside of your protagonist's world.

Your sidekick usually needs to be a simple character, and is typically not a good source for subplots. While the sidekick may have a developed backstory, her allegiance to the protagonist is total and she is motivated by loyalty. A subplot for the sidekick runs the risk of splitting her interests and loyalty, thus making her a less trustworthy character.

The guide is also typically a simple character, though subplots are more common around this character. Your reader must trust that the guide is truthful to a fault. Unlike the sidekick, the guide is not motivated by loyalty to the protagonist, but by loyalty to the cause. The guide is the arbiter of right and wrong, just and unjust, possible and impossible. Any subplot around the guide should reflect his position.

Morpheus in *The Matrix* is a great example of the guide subplot. Morpheus's story, the one he's a protagonist of, is that he's been looking for "The One" and believes that he's destined to find the messiah character. Morpheus is more loyal to his beliefs than he ever is to Neo, and that is always at the center of the actions Morpheus takes and the subplot points that he develops. The subplot reinforces his characterization as the guide.

Your frenemy, however, *must* have elaborate interests. This character is untrustworthy, whether by loyalty or incompetence, and introduces variables to the plot. This character is not motivated by loyalty to the protagonist. So what does motivate him? What competing interest could make him flip at the most or least opportune time?

Similarly, your object of affection usually doesn't care at all for the main character, or at least doesn't operate in the interest of the pro-tagonist. The Object just gets in trouble because he's pursuing some-thing else. So what else is he pursuing? Why?

## APPLYING SUBPLOTS

Once you've identified some subplots that you want to include in your work, now you can apply them to story structure. Simply identify scenes and minor plot points as needed that will serve the subplots through the story.

However, note that most subplots will require *no new scenes*. In fact, good subplots feel more like character development than they do like tell-ing a story. Your reader will learn and understand the subplots through the character development in the scenes that serve your primary plot and conflicts. A few extra words embedded in dialogue will often do the trick.

For instance, your frenemy may make a reference that he just came from the hospital for his wife's chemotherapy treatment. You've seeded a subplot. That subplot can continue to be developed through little offhanded comments that tell the reader what's happening "off-stage". You're building a more robust world, you're giving the charac-ter depth, and your reader is smart enough to piece together small data points into a rich side story. You could build a whole subplot about the frenemy's wife's cancer, yet the reader never "sees" the wife and never visits the hospital.

Han Solo owes money to the gangster Jabba the Hut. This subplot is built with no scenes added. The entire subplot is developed in dialogue that relates to the core plot and conflicts, with only one short extension of the cantina scene in which Han is confronted by and shoots an alien bounty hunter named Greedo. Note that the audience was already in the cantina with Luke, the existing scene has only been extended.

In the 1997 re-mastering, the studio added in a computer-animat-ed scene of Jabba the Hut that was shot but not included in the original movie. It's a cool moment for *Star Wars* buffs to see Jabba earlier in the franchise, but the scene stands out as contrived. It only serves the subplot. The editors were right to cut it from the original.

Subplots carry a *duty to maintain*. When you introduce new sub-plots, you plant a seed in the reader's brain, and you then have an obligation to care for that seed. This is especially true when subplots require dedicated scenes.

This is why the bonus scene in *Star Wars* fails. We're introduced to this developed subplot with a dedicated scene, but then we never return to it. There are no more scenes which serve the subplot in the same way. A rule was established in the first half of the story that we're going to interface with Han Solo's debt story with dedicated, developed scenes, but then that rule was abandoned.

Challenge yourself: How much subplot can you develop on the backs of your existing scenes?

This won't work for all subplots. We can contrast this approach, which is by far the most common, with a story like *The Departed* or *Heat*, which each have highly developed antagonists, who each carry a developed subplot of their own.

If you're going to employ scenes that are dedicated to a subplot, then you need to consistently service that subplot with dedicated scenes throughout the manuscript.

## A LIFE OF THEIR OWN

The fun thing about subplots is that they tend to develop all on their own within the freedom of a loosely held outline. As you de-velop your characters and they interact, you'll find all kinds of neat plot elements. It's perfectly fine for minor subplots to develop in the background, just don't get excited and pursue them all. Your structure will go frenetic and you'll lose your reader's attention.

Specifically choose three to five subplots that you intend to devel-op and will commit to maintain, and make sure that those subplots are represented throughout the manuscript. Let the other subplots linger in the background without further development.

As a fun challenge that will keep your storytelling tight, how can you tell your subplots without ever leaving the main narrative, only utilizing the scenes for the primary plot? How can you add depth to your characters without ever creating an extra scene? This isn't strictly necessary or always possible, but bearing it in mind as a guideline will keep your story tight and on track.

Subplots are critical to the novel. They bring depth, complexity, and life to your characters. You'll usually get the most value from them by treating them as character development, rather than separate plot lines.

# 14

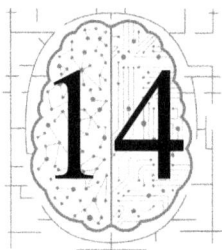

# VALIDATE AND MAKE IT GREAT

SIMPLY KNOWING THE THEORY of the Novel Matrix isn't enough. As the letter in the Bible from the Apostle James tells us, "Don't just be hearers of the word, be doers of the word." (my own paraphrase)

So it's time to apply this. Before you write a single word, you're going to create a plan for the story you intend to tell. You're going to use the included worksheets, and you're going to conceptualize the whole story.

Our ideal is to write a specific story on purpose—a story that you chose and developed before the first words hit the page.

DOWNLOAD FULL-SIZE WORKSHEETS

FREE RESOURCES AT NOVELMATRIX.COM

When you've assigned all the Novel Matrix elements, no more—no less, then you can move forward with the confidence that your novel will "work" and that it will be neither "too fat" nor "too skinny."

You can fill out these worksheets in any order, and all at the same time. All of these elements interrelate, so there's no set order to fill them out. You'll fill in a little bit here and a little bit there until it's all done.

Your characters will influence your conflicts, your conflicts will influence your plot, your plot will have bearing on your story's universe. We can identify these ingredients individually, but we can never fully separate them from one another. On the contrary, we actually want the elements to all intersect and reinforce each other.

When planning your novel, start with what you know. Perhaps you have an inspiration for a really cool protagonist, a spectacular setting, or a plot twist at the Climax. Start with what you know, and fill it in.

You may simply know that there's an issue you want to talk about—abortion, the second amendment, globalism, or clean food—if that's the case, fill in the philosophical conflicts first.

It doesn't matter. Fill in what you know, and then work out from there.

You'll work through the rest of the process until all of the pieces fit together.

Hold the plan with a loose hand until all of the pieces reinforce and harmonize with each other. You may end up identifying and then erasing some elements several times. That's all part of the process. Aren't you glad you're doing it now, rather than *after* you've written 30,000 words that all need to change?

I look at this process like a Japanese sliding block puzzle. You know, the kind where there's a grid with one open square, and you can only move one block at a time to bring the puzzle together. In the same way, we're defining, shifting, and redefining elements until it all fits just right.

It's a challenge to make all of the pieces fit well, but it's also an opportunity. Let the individual pieces influence and inspire each other.

When you're stuck in one area, look for the answer in another section of the plan. For instance, if you can't figure out an Icarus Moment, look to your conflicts. Which Little World conflict is the most important? What kind of event would draw that most into focus?

If you can't figure out who the sidekick character will be, look through your plot and conflicts to see if there's some specific kind of help the protagonist will need.

If you're struggling with the Little World philosophical conflict, take some time to develop your frenemy and your guide. What do they believe? Are their worldviews in contrast? If not, can they be? Is there another character that brings an opposing philosophy to the story?

This kind of thinking not only solves the blank spots in your plan, but it also ensures that you weave the pieces together. Ideally, every piece reinforces all the others.

This process will take some time. If you are very inspired, perhaps you could complete it in a few hours. Even so, let it sit for a few days and revisit it before you embark on writing your novel. You can certainly make changes after you begin writing and your characters surprise you, but our goal is to lock in this story concept before we begin.

## DEBUGGING THE NOVEL MATRIX

Here are a few common errors and frustrations I've encountered as I've worked with authors to implement the Novel Matrix. Before you call the plan done, make sure you've satisfied all eight of these questions:

**Question #1: Can I say the premise in one sentence? Is it impossible?**

Does your premise sound ridiculous? It should!

Every popular story you can think of sounds crazy if you summarize it in one sentence.

Farm boy becomes a starfighter pilot AND blows up the planet-killer. (*Star Wars*)

Archaeologist saves the world by rescuing the lost biblical Ark of the Covenant from the Nazis. (*Indiana Jones and the Raiders of the Lost Ark*)

A virtuous, articulate young man with a promising future is reluctantly sucked into the family crime business and rises to become the most violent crime boss ever. (*The Godfather*)

A plucky, self-centered billionaire overcomes his narcissism to assemble a team and thwarts a Russian terrorist. (*Iron Man 2*)

The thing that the protagonist is going to do should be absolutely ridiculous in the beginning. If we're just looking at the character in the first chapter, the reader should feel like the task is utterly impossible. Over the course of 60,000 words, you're going to make the impossible possible. If the goal isn't impossible for the hero to achieve on page one, then it's not hard enough—make it more absurd.

By the same token, you should be able to describe your book in one sentence. You should have one driving storyline that your protagonist will follow. If you're having trouble identifying just one sentence, look at your five conflicts and put a square around the most important conflict that you will completely resolve. That's your Driving Conflict and is the key to your story.

Your single story sentence should not just be a premise, it should also include the ending.

## Question #2: Is the protagonist actually doing anything, or just making a decision to do something?

Deciding to be the hero is not a sufficient resolution.

When my apprentices craft novel outlines, I hear this often, *the protagonist goes through a journey and in the Climax, he decides that he'll be the hero, that he'll step into the call.*

That's not enough to carry the story. Very likely the protagonist will make that decision at some point in the manuscript. Usually in the Rock Bottom moment the protagonist will begin to exercise "agency" and step into the call, however, that can't be the whole book.

Imagine if Frodo spent a whole book just deciding whether or not to take on the ring. (OK, in fairness, it *does* take us about 30,000 words to get there.)

Imagine if Michael Corleone took an entire movie just to decide to step into the crime family.

What if Hitch's climax was that he'd finally give dating a try?

That would all be boring. In each of those stories, it's a huge plot point that the character decides to step into the mission. However, it's not enough. What we really want to see is what happens after the big decision. Now that they've said, "yes," what happens next?

The protagonist decides he'll be the hero…so what?

If you find yourself with three acts that just climax with the character making a hard decision, here's your solution: shrink your plot sequence.

Simply move everything back and make your Climax into your Icarus Moment. Now that the protagonist has decided he'll be the hero, get back in the dating game, or take on the challenge, then what is he going to do about it? And since it's now your Icarus Moment, how are the bad guys going to absolutely smack him off of his newly self-appointed pedestal?

Refer back to Question #1, what ridiculous thing will he accomplish now that he's said "yes"?

## Question #3: Are all five conflicts actually different things?

Sometimes we end up with different versions of the same idea in all five conflict boxes.

For example, the internal conflict includes the protagonist's desire to please her mother. The external conflict is the protagonist against her mother. And the philosophical conflict is about the role of mothers.

It's all the same thing. The story will be just as thin as if we only had one conflict.

This is a little bit of a balancing act. In a well-constructed story with thematic irony, there will be some crossover between conflicts, they'll share *some* similar ideas. However, while we want the borders to touch, make sure you also have diversity.

Oftentimes this can be solved simply by developing each side of the conflict into more specific defensible ideas. Look at what you're starting with and then ask the question, "How? Why?" If one side of your Little World internal conflict is "Sally wants to please her mother," perhaps that can be developed to "Sally wants to prove to her mother that she can succeed in a professional career," or "Sally wants to please her mother by finding a good man to marry."

You'll achieve more distinction by becoming *more* specific in your plan.

Work with those questions and force yourself to make the Little World internal conflict and the Little World philosophical conflict very different from each other.

This issue is especially pervasive in stories that are primarily motivated by an internal conflict, which brings us to the issue of the missing antagonist.

## Question #4: Where's the antagonist?

Especially in genres like literary fiction, you may at first struggle to identify a real antagonist. Ironically, the mega-antagonist is usually easier to identify in these genres. We can usually identify some systemic evil easily enough, but finding a real person who actually cares to confront the protagonist's journey can be more challenging.

Remember that the antagonist should be an actual, literal person. The antagonist shouldn't be an idea, and it can't be the protagonist herself. Of course the protagonist is her own worst enemy (aren't we all?), but we still need someone on the page that the audience can see and relate to and who will manifest those conflicts.

What crazy thing is the protagonist going to do? It's not just action heroes who do impossible things. Real people do impossible things every day. Real people conquer PTSD. They break addictions. They overcome fear. They give up the things that are most important to them in order to step into a greater calling. These things are impossible! That's why they're worth writing stories about.

If you can't identify an Impossible Thing (as is sometimes the case with memoirs, for example), then why are you telling this story? We may need to be realistic and decide that this particular story idea isn't a great candidate for a novel-length work.

When we've identified the Impossible Thing, the antagonist usually comes to us more easily. The antagonist is the person who is going to make that mission more difficult for the protagonist.

There are two ways that we commonly see the antagonist operate. The antagonist can stand directly opposed to the protagonist's goal, like Darth Vader has a vested interest is seeing the Death Star *not* blow up. Or, the antagonist wants the same thing as the protagonist, and they can't both have it.

In *Raiders of the Lost Ark*, Belloq wants to find the Ark of the Covenant just as much as Indiana does. The universe dictates that there's no way they can work together—only one of them can have it.

Who stands in the way of your protagonist's Impossible Thing? Or, who wants the same thing as your protagonist, and it seems (at least to the protagonist) like they can't both have it?

**Question #5: Am I sufficiently ruining my protagonist's life?**

Sometimes coming up with the Impossible Thing that the protagonist will accomplish, the high point of the story, is easy. Sometimes we have trouble making the protagonist's life terrible enough for the low parts.

Kurt Vonnegut's sixth rule of writing is, "Be a sadist. No matter how sweet and innocent your leading characters, make awful things happen to them, in order that the reader may see what they are made of."

Remember that we have to crush the protagonist. She can't get a little bit down. We need to take her to her literal worst day. Not just a really bad day, she needs to seemingly permanently lose everything that's most important to her. We need to see what's underneath of her skin.

The antagonist is going to help with that, and you should look there first. But that's not always enough, especially in the beginning of the story.

Add injustice. Make something just absolutely unfair happen to the protagonist.

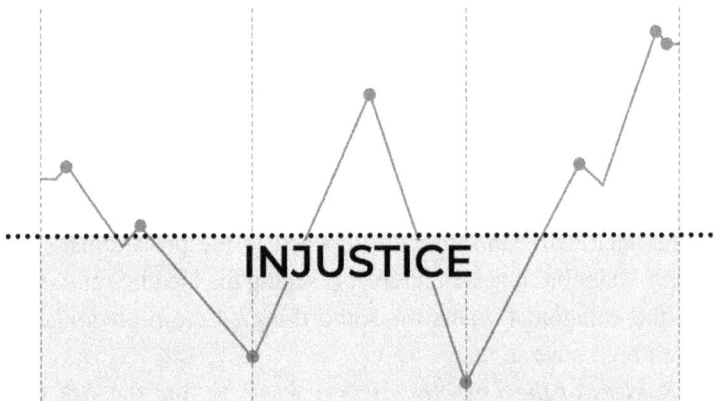

INJUSTICE

In the first act, the bar for *deus ex machina* is extremely low, so random bad stuff can just happen as long as it's consistent with the universe. A wildfire can burn down the family home. The parents can get shot in a mugging gone wrong. The protagonist can be accused of a crime he didn't commit. The spouse can cheat. The car can break down. An airliner can crash into the barn. Scandals can erupt. Identity thieves can strike... You get the idea. You can do anything, just make it unfair.

On the downward side of the second act, the events have to have a more established relationship to the plot, but the same idea applies. This is when your frenemy (or someone else) will actually or seemingly betray the protagonist. So unfair!

Maybe the tools that the protagonist collected turn out to be fakes or just plain don't work. So unfair!

How is the mega-antagonist going to crush the protagonist in the second act? The protagonist should have raised the ire of the systemic-level bad guy, how will that bad guy use his vast resources to absolutely mistreat the protagonist?

**Question #6: Is my protagonist too perfect?**

The other way to thrust your protagonist way down is to focus on his imperfections. Too often our impulse is to write protagonists that don't make bad decisions. That's an incorrect understanding of the "good guy."

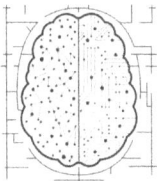

Your protagonist is likely a *good person*, which means that he has good intentions. He's *usually trying* to act with integrity, and we can support his big goals. But your protagonist can't be perfect. Sometimes he really has to screw up.

The solution is not more trauma

What's wrong with your good guy? I'm not asking what trauma your protagonist is carrying. *The solution is not more backstory trauma.* I'm asking, on his best day, what are his shortcomings?

Has your protagonist made bad decisions? Let him participate in his own destruction!

Is he lazy? Forgetful? Not so smart? Distractible? Childish? Insensitive? A little bit crass?

The list goes on, but what are his normal-type shortcomings? Again, we're not talking he's missing a limb or he goes comatose when he hears the ocean (ever since the incident), we're talking about the normal stuff of being a human.

You're good at some things and with other things you fall short. Your protagonist is the same.

I'm a super direct person. Depending on the situation it's either my greatest asset or my worst liability.

I try to do everything myself. I'm not afraid to ask for help, I just struggle to trust other people to do as good of a job as I know I will do.

Believe me, I could go on, but you get the idea. If you're not sure, make a list about yourself. Then make a list for your protagonist.

Ironically, when your protagonist makes honest mistakes, she will actually become more likable. Sometimes we're afraid to disappoint our reader. It turns out that our readers have shortcomings too, and they relate to other humans who aren't perfect.

If your reader isn't sometimes

NEED SOME IDEAS?

CHECK OUT:
"21 WAYS TO RUIN YOUR PROTAGONIST'S LIFE (WITHOUT COMPROMISING THEIR MORALITY)"

saying, "Why would you do that?! That's so stupid?!" then your protagonist may need a more obvious shortcoming.

How about your secondary characters? Remember that your sidekick should be unquestionably loyal and generally effective for the protagonist, but the sidekick can still have reasonable human shortcomings and make mistakes.

## Question #7: What's driving my protagonist?

In the first act, we're going to put the protagonist in a position where inaction is no longer an option. She either needs to decide to stand up and fight for what's right or she needs to roll over and give up. If she gave up, we wouldn't bother to tell the story (because it lacks an Impossible Thing), so we're assuming that she's going to buckle up and do the hard thing.

But how do we get her moving in the right direction?

Injustice and the protagonist's shortcomings move the story arc *down*. What are our mechanisms for driving the story *up*?

Your first tool is the guide. The guide helps the protagonist identify the mission. The protagonist doesn't always have to follow the advice (and this may be one of those reasonable character defects that wrecks her life), but *eventually* the protagonist has to get on board with the guide's counsel.

If the guide is no longer present in the story, she can still have influence. The protagonist may remember her counsel, encounter her in a dream or vision, or find an artifact that brings the advice home (like a journal, video clip, or even a souvenir).

What's one reason the protagonist takes action? Because the guide said so.

The object of affection is also a tool for positive action. When your protagonist needs a reason to move forward, make your object of affection do something stupid (again) and need saved. Incidentally, this works whether you're trying to move in a positive or negative direction, it'll just get you moving forward. The protagonist can walk into a trap or stumble upon a solution.

Place your object of affection where your protagonist needs to be in order to serve your plot. This is why in most traditional stories the object of affection is also the romantic interest. The girl gets captured by the bad guy, which places the protagonist and the antagonist on a collision course. The protagonist can no longer accomplish the Impossible Thing by bypassing the antagonist. Now they have to fight.

This works exactly the same outside of an action/adventure context. Place the object of affection where you need the fireworks to go off. When your protagonist comes running…showtime.

**Question #8: How is this a story of agency?**

An elephant stood tethered to a pole by a small rope—just a little piece of string to hold a 2,000 pound elephant. The elephant stretched to try to reach some hay on the edge of the circle, but the tiny rope held her back with the hay just beyond reach.

A visitor asked the keeper, "Why doesn't she break the rope?" The keeper answered, "We put the rope on her when she was very young and she could not break it. She learned that she could not break it and still believes it."

We are all that elephant in one way or another.

We are all contained by systems and we believe in our own limitations, whether that containment is real or imagined. We all know the feeling of being trapped and unable to reach our potential.

In what ways is your protagonist "trapped" in the first act? Is she really trapped, or does she simply believe that she's trapped?

Is your protagonist's cage real, or has she accepted some kind of imaginary limitation? In what ways will she exercise agency and fail in the second act, but find success in the third act?

Stories of agency instantly connect with readers, even if they're not interested in the subject matter. We all know what it feels like to be trapped by our circumstances, unable to self-determine the future.

Let your readers see the elephant break the rope and they'll love you for it.

## IDENTIFY YOUR TARGET READER

Kurt Vonnegut's seventh rule of writing is, "Write to please just one person. If you open a window and make love to the world, so to speak, your story will get pneumonia."

Who are you writing this story for? Don't describe a type of person—is there

HOW TO IDENTIFY YOUR AUDIENCE:

FREE RESOURCE AT NOVELMATRIX.COM

one specific person that you could name, other than yourself, whom you would like to enjoy this story?

Practically no story will be interesting to everyone. Choose one person, and make sure that they would absolutely eat it up.

Tell your story in one sentence. Then tell it in three sentences.

Would those three sentences absolutely grab that one specific reader, gut her, and leave her wanting more?

## FROM GOOD TO GREAT

Hallmark is living proof that you can use this structure to write good stories that fall short of greatness. Before we're too hard on Hallmark, let's remember that it's a paying gig for everybody involved.

Lots of really good authors are writing good books, doing what they love, and getting paychecks. They may not go down in history as great minds of literature or influencers of culture, but there is nothing wrong with living your dreams, having fun, and getting paid. Most of us will be forgotten in a hundred years.

However, you may aspire for more.

There are many factors that can draw a manuscript from goodness to greatness. The Novel Matrix is a vehicle that automatically starts you at "good." It's up to you to grow in your artistry and exceptionalism in the craft to take the story to greatness. But good or great, the Novel Matrix is at the core.

Read books critically.

Read poorly written books and figure out why they're bad.

Read amazing books, but instead of falling in love with them, pick them apart until you know why they tick and even where they fall short.

Read successful books in genres you wouldn't normally seek out and challenge yourself to figure out why they work for that particular audience.

Challenge yourself to analyze books as a story mechanic, rather than as a consumer of story.

If most writers are using the same structures, which they are, then how do they surprise you? Read the greats, read the worsts, and do it all through the lens of craft and mechanics.

Like any tool, the Novel Matrix requires practice. You'll get better at it the more you use it.

I've helped hundreds of authors apply these ideas. Usually, the first plan isn't a winner. It takes a few plans to really make the pieces fit.

Before you commit to writing any project, challenge yourself to make several complete plans. Practice engineering stories before you fall in love with your idea.

With these tools in your belt and a little practice, you're going to be pumping out comprehensive story ideas in no time.

With just a sliver of an idea—just one single square on the plan—you'll be able to fill out the plan around it and develop that little spark into a roaring fire.

The Novel Matrix is a platform so that you can affect hearts and minds. You have things that you want to say about the world. Story is your vehicle for sharing truth. The Novel Matrix will make sure that story starts every time you turn the key.

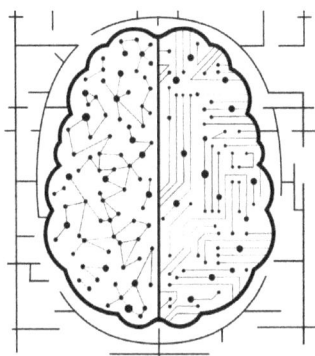

# PART III
# DOING THE WORK

# 15

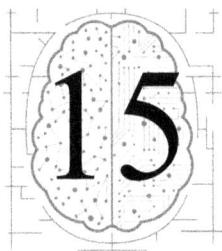

# THE WORK OF
# WRITING A NOVEL

THOUSANDS OF YEARS ago, Aristotle observed the three-act structure. It wasn't contrived or manipulated, it was something that seemed to evolve of its own accord, something that intersected with the way humans were made to understand story.

Just like Aristotle, we're not inventing these critical story elements as some kind of prescription for success. Rather, we've simply observed what the vast majority of successful storytellers do, often without even knowing they're doing it.

Just like a hot rod needs to have an engine, a transmission, wheels, and seats to be a hot rod, your story needs a universe, a plot structure, conflict, and characters in order to be a story. We are simply describing what a novel-length story is.

So often, new novelists try to create something before they even understand what it is they're trying to create. A "novel" is not just 200 pages of consecutive words. It's a specific art form with intuitive, but not always obvious, parameters and expectations.

We haven't fabricated these ideas out of thin air. Not only can we observe them over and over again in successful stories, but they also match human psychology. We were made to live in story, to under-stand the world around us in story, and to engage with story. There is a meeting point between reality and how our brains are designed to understand story, and the Novel Matrix describes the intersection.

In addition to shaping our understanding of the art form, the Novel Matrix also turns this great, nebulous, creative task into predictable labor.

## WRITING IS WORK

Dave Ramsey, who has helped millions of people get out of debt, likes to say that paying off your debt is about psychology as much as numbers. Your household finances are not just a math puzzle, it's equally or more about what's happening inside of your head and your heart.

The same is true of writing a book. Getting the right information is an important first step, but so much of your success will come down to your attitude and how you understand the work of the project.

The key I'm about to share with you is as important as everything else I've shared so far. As much as success in writing is about excel-lent story theory, prose craft, and character development, it's equally important to come to healthy terms with this truth:

### Writing is work.

That doesn't mean it can't be fun. That doesn't mean it's not in-spired. However, we need to dispel the romantic idea that writing is some sort of intangible art form. You do not have to serve at the whim of the muse.

In my extensive experience, this singular concept is the difference between successful authors and amateur writers. Some of the most brilliant, gifted writers I know will never produce anything because they can't accept this premise. Meanwhile, some of the hackiest writ-ers I know are influencing readers and getting paychecks because one way or the other they're getting words on the page. They're doing the work and releasing books.

## EVERY WRITING PROJECT IS A FINITE AMOUNT OF WORK

There are a particular number of hours standing between you and a finished manuscript. You may not yet know exactly how many hours that is, but the fact is that there is a specific number.

My kids love Legos, like most kids do. Sometimes when they play, they get Lego blocks everywhere. Somehow little bitty pieces scatter the floor in an eight-foot radius from wherever they're playing. Little blocks, wheels, levers, tiny heads are embedded in the carpet, lying in wait for some night I'm walking through the house barefoot in the dark.

When my kids need to clean up, the task can feel insurmountable. There are so many pieces to pick up. It seems endless. "We can't do it," they cry, "it's too much."

But that's not true.

The fact is that there are a specific number of Lego blocks on the floor. We might not know the number. It could be a hundred, two hundred, eight hundred, ten thousand. Who knows? But there is a specific number. The Legos can't spawn new Legos. No more can arrive. There's a set number.

That means that if we diligently pick up one little block at a time and put it back in the bucket, eventually they'll all be put away. Every block that we put away means that there's one less on the floor. That's the only way it works.

My kids can sit on the floor overwhelmed, complaining about the task and feeling like *it's just too much*. Or they can start moving, one handful at a time, and they'll be done in less time than they spent complaining.

Your novel project is no different. There is a finite amount of work between you and a complete manuscript.

One of the most helpful things about the Novel Matrix is that it helps us to understand the process of writing a novel as finite work. There aren't endless possibilities and vast unknown variables, there are certain tasks that you're going to perform in a logical order, and then it will be done.

It may be a very large number of tasks. We may not know the exact number of tasks. Especially if this is your first novel project, you may have no idea what that work feels like or how to estimate the effort it takes. But nonetheless, there is a specific amount of work that needs to be done, and then your project will be complete.

Every time you complete a task, there is one less task to be completed.

This may seem elementary. But accepting this premise in your heart is critical to your success.

Novel manuscripts only become infinite when they're not appropriately planned. For the pantser without any plan, it's true that any task you complete may indeed create more tasks. The process may very well be unending.

We're trained to believe that art is this magical, nebulous thing that can't be harnessed. *We're subject to the muse, we can only do it when inspiration strikes.*

But that's not how successful novelists behave.

You are the muse. Conjuring up your creativity on demand is a skill that you can develop.

Successful artists have learned to make art into work. That might not sound like quite as much fun, but it's reality.

With the Novel Matrix, you can write a novel in 100 hours. Because you've taken time to order your steps, you can apply your labor diligently and predictably. Because you haven't overplanned, you can still have fun and surprise yourself while you do it.

## WRITING AS A HOBBY

I smoke meats for fun. It's an art and I enjoy it. Sometimes I do it a lot, other times there'll be months between times that I wheel out the smoker and fire it up. I enjoy experimenting, and I even try to do my best at it and improve. I read about it, I watch videos, I talk with other people who share my hobby. I hope that each brisket or pork loin is better than the last one.

But I don't have any illusions that I'm going to start a restaurant or go win the top prize at the Columbus Jazz and Ribs Fest.

If you just want to have fun with your writing, just write for fun. When you feel inspired, sit down for an hour and tap away at the keys. Take stuff to your local writing group. Share writing memes online. Give a beat poem at open mic. Wear a fedora or a cape if you want. Buy a fancy writing notebook and a coffee cup that says something ironic on it. Work on something for a few weeks, and then when it's not fun anymore put it aside.

I mean this quite seriously. There's absolutely nothing wrong with writing as a hobby because it's fun.

But then recognize it for what it is.

You can't act that way and at the same time seriously expect to see your name on the bestseller list someday or expect to quit your job and write full-time.

If you want to write professionally, it will require a different mindset. If you have aspirations in your heart to excel at the craft and have success in the market, then you'll need to treat it like professional work.

This is true of any art form. Art is for everyone (and everyone should do it!), but to do it as a professional requires a different mindset. Professional painters, musicians, filmmakers, chefs, and so many others understand that in order to achieve exceptionalism and make money with their craft, they need to treat it like work. They do it on the days even when they don't want to.

I also like to play guitar. I regularly lead worship with small groups, and I really enjoy it. I have little talent but medium practiced skills. These days I practice when I want to, which is basically never. When I play, I'm rarely trying to get better, I just play what I know. People seem to appreciate it and enjoy it. I think Jesus likes it. I don't have any fantasies or aspirations for it. So I can do whatever I want with it.

Maybe I could do more with it if I really wanted to. I bet I could if I put my mind to it. But I don't love it. I'm not passionate about it. When I think about practicing every day, doing shows, and promoting myself doing that, I get a big old pile of *nah* in my tummy. Is that how you feel about your writing?

This might be an epiphany moment for you.

There's a lot of money to be made out there in the writing community telling everyone to follow their dreams. Just keep trying. Don't give up. You're a writer no matter what.

But let's get real. If this idea of doing it every day, challenging yourself to get better, subjecting yourself to hard criticism, promoting your work…if your reaction to all of that is "no thanks," then maybe you don't want to be a professional writer. And that's okay.

You can still write. You can still use the Novel Matrix and write a book. You may even surprise yourself. But do it without the pressure. Temper the aspirations and just enjoy writing. You'll have so much more fun that way.

If you're not just the weekend grill master and you're ready to put in the time, work, and dedication it takes to write a book, keep going. If you're willing to turn this art that you love into a predictable and consistent work, then stick with me.

After working with hundreds of authors to produce books, I can tell you with certainty that the biggest barrier to success isn't creativity, talent, originality, or even connections. The biggest determinant in your success is work ethic.

Your ability to develop a discipline of writing will be your biggest asset. If you're intent on being a writer, you'll write a lot of books. Some of them will end up in the trash and others will end up in bookstores. Only by producing real work in real quantities will you really learn your voice and find your way in the marketplace.

We've had some fun with the theory of novels, and we've taken the time to plan a well-devised story. Now it's time to put that to work.

# 16

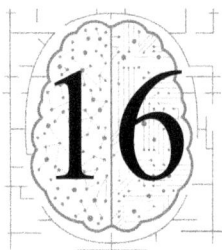

# BUILDING A SCENE LIST

PLANTSING IS THE SOLUTION. Planning, but not overplanning, gives you a workable story so that you can move forward with confidence, work even when you're not inspired, and push through self-doubt. Plantsing works out the story but leaves enough wiggle room that you can still have fun, surprise yourself, and allow parts of the story and character to develop as you go.

After you've developed the core elements of your story with a Novel Matrix plan, we're going to use that information to create a scene list.

A *scene* is a complete unit of story. It is usually a sequence of unbroken action which occurs in a specific time and place. In most cases, when the story breaks and jumps to a new time and place, we would consider that a different scene. Scenes and chapters are not the same thing. Some authors break their chapters at every scene, other authors include more than one scene per chapter. There is no rule on the matter.

In some cases, you may include multiple locations or character sets in a scene, but nonetheless, there's something that ties it all together to make it a complete unit of story.

To begin building a scene list at the most basic level, look through your plot structure, what needs to happen to motivate your protagonist from one major plot point to the next? Anything that the reader needs to see your protagonist doing is a scene.

As your protagonist drives from one plot point to the next, we also need to service the other elements of your plan. Each of your characters and each of your conflicts needs space in the book. If your plot focuses on the protagonist's external conflict, where are some logical places to inject a scene that will draw out and show her internal conflict as well?

A scene list is exactly what it sounds like. You're just going to make a simple list of scenes in order, with a few brief details about each one.

## EVERY SCENE SERVES THE STORY

Have you noticed that no one ever goes to the bathroom or eats a sandwich in a story unless it serves some purpose (usually comedic)? Your reader is very smart and he is exceptionally good at filling in the blanks.

Consider the following sequence of events:

- A man and a woman are sitting three seats away from each other other on a bus, seemingly unaware of the other. The man turns and catches her eye.

- The same man and woman sit across from each other at a table in a quaint coffee shop.

- The woman is in a wedding dress walking down a path through a nicely mowed field. The man waits in a tuxedo under a gazebo.

- The woman cradles a baby in her arms.

With just four data points, you have very likely put together a complete story. A man and a woman met on a bus, fell in love, got married, and had a baby.

You probably haven't had a tremendous emotional connection, but you would if we developed these four scenes. Just limiting ourselves to these four incidents, I could make you cry simply by developing these characters into real people.

There's so much we don't know. But you put the pieces together.

We didn't see an escalating series of dates or even a single meal. We didn't see a proposal. We didn't see a honeymoon. We don't know whose home they decided to keep. We don't even know how long it's been. Nonetheless, you were able to put the pieces together.

Now let's add a few more scenes to the same sequence of events:

- A car crashes in the woods.

- The same man, dressed in a black suit, weeps alone over a headstone in the cemetery.

- The man walks through the park holding the hand of a little boy.

Are you still keeping up with the story? Of course you are!

When it comes to scenes, less is more. Your readers are very smart and are able to piece the story together even more effectively than you can tell it. They need you to bring the characters to life and guide the ship, but they'll fill in so much in their imagination. Focus on the key events where things change or that illustrate an important element of the story.

Every single scene should develop character, motivate the plot, and develop themes. If a scene doesn't accomplish at least two of these things, cut it. Be ruthless.

This is what is meant by the phrase "kill your darlings." It's not actually about killing off your characters. What it means is to eliminate elements that don't serve the story, even if you really love those things or it was the coolest idea ever. Set it aside, maybe there will be a more appropriate project for that idea later.

If a scene, paragraph, or sentence is not accomplishing the work of the story, it has go.

## RAISE THE STAKES

Every scene should raise the stakes or intentionally provide relief by resolving something at stake. There is no middle ground. Even when the protagonist is "winning," the reader should see that she's getting herself into an even deeper mess, that the results of failure would be even more catastrophic than we previously imagined.

Don't forget to establish positive stakes as well as negative ones.

Falling into a ten-foot deep hole from the ground hurts. Falling into a ten-foot hole from atop a ten-foot ladder hurts a lot more. Threatening the protagonist with bad outcomes is great, simultaneously having her at risk of losing something amazing is even better.

The action of the story provides stakes, but the universe itself is also an important way that you develop the stakes. In the universe of your story, what happens to people who are making the moral compromises your protagonist is considering?

Make sure that you're *demonstrating* the rules of the universe (as in, *showing*). Don't simply explain the consequences, let your reader see another character experiencing them. Don't tell us that the king hangs thieves, instead let your protagonist walk by a dead man swinging on the gallows.

## PRESERVE THE FREEDOM MARGIN

When you make a scene list, you're not trying to dictate every minor detail of the story in your planning. We're establishing some guide rails for the story. It's advisable to leave yourself some room to play.

For instance, you may plan that in one scene the characters have to travel through the haunted forest and in the process re-establish their bond of brotherhood. But you don't have to decide exactly how that's going to happen. As you come to that scene and are inspired, you can decide if they're going to have an argument or a fist fight, or if they're going to encounter some mutual foe that requires them to work together. As you write and feel the vibe, you can decide what kind of haunted forest this is.

You don't need to plan every detail—give yourself space to be surprised. The important thing about the planning stage is that we've carefully designated a purpose to each scene. You know in advance what a scene needs to accomplish and why it's important to the story you're telling.

## CHECK ALL THE BOXES

Every element of your Novel Matrix plan needs to be represented in the scene list.

Are all five conflicts touched upon periodically? A scene can certainly serve more than one conflict, but are there specific moments in which your internal, external, and philosophical conflicts will be developed?

Are all of your characters maintained? Are there gaps in the scene list where a character doesn't show up for a *long* time and there's no good reason for it?

Which scenes will *show* elements of the universe, and help the reader to understand the rules, long before those rules become important to the action of the story?

## DEVELOPING A SCENE

Every scene should have a driving idea. After you identify it, ask yourself if the idea requires a whole scene.

For example: "The protagonist travels to St. Louis."

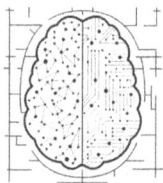

If you can eliminate a whole scene with one sentence, do it.

Unless something else important happens on the trip, this doesn't require a scene. You can establish the change of location with a single line of dialogue.

What else does this scene accomplish? Is there something that will be important to the story later that happens on his trip? Does something happen in this timespan that seriously develops the character? If not, cut the scene. Build this information into the next scene instead.

If you can eliminate a whole scene with one sentence, do it.

"Brad stepped into the cab at the St. Louis airport. 'My connecting flight from Chicago ran late. Take me to the closest bad guys, and step on it,' he said as he handed the driver a hundred dollar bill."

There, I just eliminated at least three airports and two airplanes.

If the character was bored on the flight, your reader would have been too.

Every scene should accomplish at least two of the following things:

- Move the plot forward

- Develop characters

- Reinforce themes

For each scene, write your answer to these questions on a notecard or a page in a 3-ring binder:

- What is the purpose of this scene?

- How does this scene move the plot forward?

- Which conflicts does this scene service?

- Which character(s) will this scene develop or maintain?

- Does this scene raise the stakes or provide dramatic relief? How?

- What subplots will this scene develop or maintain?

- Is there an overarching thematic idea or voice to this scene?

- What changes in this scene?

*Scrivener also has some built in resources for creating scene cards like these ones.*

You may not have a specific answer for every question for every scene. How-

DOWNLOADABLE
SCENE PLAN:

FREE RESOURCE AT
NOVELMATRIX.COM

ever, every scene should be able to answer most of these questions, and none of these questions should be ignored for several scenes in a row. If you're not able to answer a particular question for this scene, make sure you're hitting it in the next one.

Approach every scene from the premise of *showing*, not *telling*. I don't want you to tell me that the character is a hypochondriac, I want to see him checking his temperature every hour and looking at the back of his throat in the mirror with a flashlight.

I don't want you to tell me that the character traveled to St. Louis, I want to see him leaving a flower store and seeing the famous arch from the parking lot.

I don't want you to tell me that light overcomes darkness, instead I want you to describe the scenery in such a way that subtly reinforces that idea in my mind.

After you write your first draft, revisit each scene with these same questions in mind. It's okay if your answers changed in the course of the writing, that freedom is good. But in your freedom, make sure you didn't leave anything out or end up with a cool scene that just doesn't serve the story. You will undoubtedly find scenes that fall short of your best intentions. Cut them out.

Even if they're super cool.

## HOW MANY SCENES?

The number of scenes that your story needs will be a function of the story you're telling, the genre, and your voice as a writer.

Ideally, you've written a short story or two before you tackle a novel. If you haven't, take some time now to do some writing. It's just a good idea to work out the kinks in your writing before you begin a major project, and it will also give you an opportunity to learn some things about yourself.

What length of scenes do you naturally write? You're a unique writer with your own personality, do you tend to write long, detailed scenes, or do you tend to write tight, fast scenes?

Ultimately, you could tell the same story with 100 quick scenes, or twenty deep dives. The tone of the story would be very different, but we could express the same story content. Neither is right or wrong.

500-1,000 word scenes will feel short and fast. 2,500+ word scenes will feel deep and slow. In addition to your natural tendency as a writer, what mood are you going for? Do you want your reader to feel like things are really moving quickly, or do you want your reader to feel like they have permission to settle into the scene and marinate there?

When in doubt, 1,000-1,500 word scenes are a great target. That's long enough to give you an opportunity to develop each scene to a reasonable depth, without giving you too much space to bog the reader down in flowery language or irrelevant details.

Once you have an idea of your voice and pace, simply divide your target word count by the average length of scene you expect.

If you like to write long 3,000 word scenes, then you'll need about twenty to complete a novel-length 50,000-80,000 word book. If you like to write quick 500 word scenes, you'll need about 100 of them.

When in doubt, about fifteen scenes per act is a good target, or about forty-five scenes all together.

## WHAT ABOUT CHAPTERS?

A chapter can be a single scene or a collection of scenes. Just like with the scenes themselves, short chapters tend to provide a feeling of velocity, while longer chapters tend to give an illusion of depth.

The average American reader can read about 9,000 words an hour. How frequently should they get a break?

Many thrillers and action-adventure stories tend to use short chapters. These are the books you say, "just one more chapter," a dozen times only to find that all of the sudden it's one o'clock in the morning.

When chapters are less than 1,500 words, that's just a ten minute commitment and it's easy to commit to one more…then another and another.

However, we don't always want velocity. With literary fiction, for example, we often want the reader to really stew in beautiful prose and the complexity of the interpersonal dynamics of the story. In that case, we may string multiple scenes together into each chapter.

As a general rule, keep your chapters less than 5,000 words. Chapters are a natural breaking point for your reader and it's unsettling to take a break mid-chapter. At 5,000 words, you're exceeding a half an hour of reading time per chapter, which may be a bigger commitment than your reader can make and may ultimately discourage your reader. We don't want to leave the reader saying, "I love the book, I'm just not able to get into it."

## THE SCENE LIST

The scene list is for your benefit. There's really no right or wrong way to do it.

In your initial planning, you can simply give each scene a descriptive name which reminds you of the important work the scene is supposed to do.

"Roger confronts Maddie and they fight"

"Cameron gets into a car accident"

"Meredith prank phone calls a drug dealer by accident"

As you develop those scenes, you can fill out a card/page for each one (or do this in your writing software). Jot down enough notes so that you don't forget any important details you want to include. This will also help you to jump right into your writing when you have time set aside, so you won't waste a bunch of time having to reread, figure out what's going on, or recall all of the details.

Remember, every scene must do at least two of the following things: move the plot forward, develop characters, and reinforce themes.

Armed with a complete scene list, you're ready to jump into the writing!

# 17

# THE NARRATOR

WHO'S THE MOST IMPORTANT CHARACTER in the book? Most people usually guess that it's the protagonist.

But they're wrong.

We often overlook the most important voice in the entire story. This character has more influence on the theme, tone, emphasis, and feeling than any other voice.

I'm talking about the narrator.

The narrator is the lens through which we perceive the story. If you change the voice of the narrator, you'll change the entire book.

The narrator does not need to be a literal character in the story—as in a named person that takes action. Sometimes that happens, but it's not necessary.

Nonetheless, the narrator should have a voice. The vocabulary you use, your intonation and rhythm, the way you focus on particular details will all shape the story. You should spend time thinking about the voice of the narrator. What kind of person is telling this story?

Look at the story of Batman. Every other decade has its own version of the Batman story. From the old 1960s TV show to the most recent Robert Pattinson portrayal, there are a lot of versions of this story. The character, backstory, and events of the story are roughly the same, yet each one has an entirely different feel. Tim Burton's 1989 version with Michael Keaton was colorful and eccentric. Christopher Nolan's *The Dark Knight* (2002) was broody and raw. Matt Reeves's *The Batman* (2022) was gritty, realistic, and demonic. Same story, different voices. Same idea, but you understand the story much differently depending on who is telling it.

Think of the narrator as a biased journalist. The narrator's not simply an objective observer reporting the facts, she's using adjectives and phrases that shape the reader's understanding of the story.

Commonly we think, "I'm telling the story, so it's my voice." This is not correct.

Just like the "real world" doesn't exist between the covers of your book, neither do you!

My wife is a professional photographer. She takes better pictures than I do. I really don't understand it, but if we both take a picture of the same thing, hers will look better. How is this possible, these are both pictures of real life, right?

Well, no, not exactly. A photograph, as real as it may seem, is a two-dimensional representation of something that's real. Four-dimensional reality undergoes a process to become a simplified, flat, static version of itself.

My wife intuitively and by training understands that conversion, and she's able to manipulate and capture a perspective with her photographs. Mine come out basically random. If we each take 100 shots on the same camera, forty of hers will be super cool and only a couple of mine (if I'm lucky).

Writing is exactly the same. Your voice no longer exists. It is impossible to capture reality, it is impossible to capture you. You are reproducing a facsimile of reality. You are turning a four-dimensional experience into little black shapes on wood pulp.

It's just...different. We can either let that turn out randomly, or we can understand the process and approach it with intentionality.

194

Writing is so simplistic. Think about this: in English we're missing at least an entire verb tense. There is reality that we cannot express in English words.

We have twelve tenses in English—past, present, future, and the like. We have future perfect, which describes something that in the future will have happened in the past, but has not yet happened in the present. "By this time tomorrow, I *will have eaten* all of my beef jerky." This implies that at the present moment I have beef jerky, but in the future it will be gone.

But we have no perfect future tense. It is almost impossible to clearly express something that has already been completed, but had not yet happened in the past time period we're discussing.

Consider this sentence: "My parents would later tell me that I had been adopted." We're trying to express that sometime between the action of the story and the present time, the parents told the child he had been adopted. We hinge the whole thing on the word "would" and then just try to forget about it.

That's about the best we can do, and it's clunky and mangled. Are there other realities we can't express that we don't even know about because we can't express them?! These are the kinds of things that keep me up at night.

When you write a book, the totality of who you are, the nuances of your thoughts, the context of your whole person in four dimensions is distilled down into a few thousand words on the page, and those words must be expressed within the limits of the language in which you're writing. Words on a page are necessarily more simplistic and different than "my voice" as I understand it in real time.

Great writers, through intuition and training, understand that process of reality becoming language. They are intentional in the way they capture and transmogrify human experience into written words.

Do you write, then read it later only to find that sometimes it's amazing, but other times there's just something off about it? The most likely cause of this phenomena is a failure to really consider and embrace a specific narrative voice. Just like my photos are of random quality and usually not good, a narrative voice that isn't thoughtfully planned and executed will yield results of random quality.

What does your narrator sound like? Even if you're writing objectively in the third person, the narrative voice will have character and personality that radiates through the description. Don't let that happen by chance, do it specifically. By careful consideration before you begin, you will ensure that the voice is consistent, engaging, and entertaining.

## POINT-OF-VIEW

If an electrician's truck is new and green and cool, what order do those adjectives go in? If you're like most English speakers, you probably couldn't tell me exactly how you know, but for some reason you do know that "the electrician's green new cool truck" is not correct. It just sounds weird. (Say it out loud if you don't believe me.)

You don't know why, but for some reason you know in your gut that I really ought to say, "a cool new green electrician's truck." Almost any English speaker would choose that order.

As it turns out, there is a rule for the order of adjectives. When multiple adjectives are used, they should be listed in order of opinion, size, age, shape, color, origin, material, and then purpose. We don't learn that rule in school. No one ever taught it to us. As an editor, I don't even have it memorized, I had to look it up just now. Yet we all know it.

In the same way, your readers, even the poor students, know rules of storytelling intuitively. Most of them probably couldn't ever verbalize those rules or pass a test about it, but they can feel it in their gut when an author breaks the rules.

Point-of-view (POV) is extremely important to your narrator. This is another subset of rules that most people couldn't necessarily explain to you, but they can feel it when the rules are broken. The storytelling experience will degrade if the rules aren't followed.

Unlike the order of adjectives, most of us did learn about point-of-view sometime around the ninth grade. Your English teacher probably explained that stories can be told in one of three "persons": first-, second-, or third-person point of view. Let's briefly review:

**First-person**: the narrator is telling you about her own personal experience using terms like I, me, we, and us. "I could feel my face flush as I looked into her eyes."

**Second-person**: the narrator is telling you about your experience, using the term you, as in, "You turn left and see a door, you walk through it." Unless you're writing a *Choose Your Own Adventure* novel, there's really no place for the second-person in fiction. There are some exceptions, but second-person is practically always awkward and clunky. Just don't do it.

**Third-person**: the narrator is telling a story about someone else, using terms like he she, they, and them. "They sat around drinking coffee and listening to the radio."

But when it comes to writing fiction, we also have to consider another dimension of the POV—*omniscience*. How much does the narrator know?

Our options are *limited, semi-omniscient*, and *omniscient. (*Note that these terms are not used in exactly the same way by all teachers of writing.)*

Here is how these options break down:

**Limited:** The narrator is a fly on the wall. The narrator's knowledge is limited to what can be observed with the five senses. The narrator doesn't know anyone's thoughts, feelings, or motivations. The narrator may NOT say, "Leslie didn't like George" or "Leslie was happy to be there that day," because both examples would require knowing Leslie's thoughts.

The narrator *can* say "Leslie frowned when she turned away from George," or "Leslie skipped through the front door with a smile on her face," because both of those things could be observed without knowing what Leslie is thinking.

Within a limited POV, the narrator can zoom in infinitely and control time. The narrator can see the pores on someone's nose and germs flying through the air. The narrator can observe how a bullet passes through an object in microseconds—the narrator's knowledge is perfect. The narrator just doesn't know what's happening inside of anyone's head or heart.

**Semi-Omniscient (SO)**: The narrator is "inside the head" of a limited number of characters, usually just one, but not everyone.

There is a "known" character, and the narrator can share how that person feels, her opinions, her motivations and dreams, and the things she imagines inside her own head.

Aside from the one "known" character, the thoughts, feelings, and motivations of the other characters are unknown, and the narrator is limited to what can be observed with the five senses, just like a limited narrator.

Usually, the narrator is limited to knowing only the main character's thoughts.

**Omniscient**: The narrator knows everything, including what every character is thinking and feeling, at all times. The narrator can say things like "Leslie was disgusted, but she swallowed the bite anyway," or "George yearned to reach out and comfort her."

All characters are fair game. The narrator knows everything, inside and out.

So we can combine the person and omniscience in a variety of ways. Here are the most common "voices" that you'll see in literature.

|  | 1ST | 2ND | 3RD |
|---|---|---|---|
| LIMITED |  | X | ★ |
| SEMI-OMNISCIENT | ★ | X | ★ |
| OMNISCIENT |  | X | ✓ |

### COMMON POINT-OF-VIEW

**First-Person Semi-Omniscient:** The story is told by a character who knows only his or her own thoughts. It wouldn't make sense in most cases for a first-person narrator to know everyone's thoughts, unless they're some sort of supernatural being, because that's not *how the world works*. I can guess other people's thoughts, but I can't really know.

First-person is a natural starting point for new storytellers because it's so similar to how you naturally tell stories. You don't need to think about any rules, you just tell a story how you would tell a story to your friends around a campfire.

The drawback of the first-person POV is that we can't "see" any events that are beyond what the narrator can observe. If the narrator can't see it or hear it, you can't include it. The reader can't see what the bad guy is secretly doing, unless the first-person character personally goes to that location and sees it.

For many stories this is perfectly fine, and with a fair amount of creativity you can find ways to include all kinds of things. A great workaround is that the narrator can include things that are being told to her by other characters.

First-person is also a fun voice because the reader gets to literally live inside the head of another person. The author has full license to really develop a unique voice and not hold back.

Masterful authors like Kurt Vonnegut operate in this voice, so it's certainly not just for beginners.

**Third-Person Limited:** The narrator is not a character in the story and is limited to observing the characters. When done properly, this leads to good strong writing because it forces the writer to *show* everything. The narrator can't tell you that George is sad, instead the narrator must describe George and lead you to the conclusion. "George sat with his head in his hands, pawing at his nose from time to time, and his down-turned lips matched his red eyes."

For most stories and writers, I recommend adopting this POV. It will force you to write with clarity and strength.

**Third-Person Semi-Omniscient:** In most cases, this means that the narrator is a third-party, not a character in the story. Just like a limited narrator, this narrator can only observe, but the narrator does know the main character's thoughts (and only the main character's thoughts).

This is a helpful POV, because it simulates a first-person story and draws the reader in tightly to the main character. The story feels personal. But it also give the narrator the freedom to observe events that are beyond the main character's perspective.

Like a *third-person limited* perspective, the narrator still has to do a lot of *showing*.

**Third-Person Omniscient:** The narrator is not a character in the story, and the narrator knows everyone's thoughts, feelings, and motivations. When we write without choosing a POV, this is typically what we do by default.

This POV tends to lead to very long and slow books. The issue is that you have a *duty to maintain* the omniscience. Once you establish that the narrator knows everyone's thoughts, the reader now has some expectation to know what everyone's thoughts are. Simple exchanges become pages-long encounters as we bounce from one person's head to another.

Tom Clancy commonly uses this POV. It is sometimes helpful in the types of scenes he's depicting, with international politics at stake and lots of individuals acting under false pretenses. But his books are huge and many readers find them tedious.

When choosing a POV, consider what's typical in your genre. If you're writing international military thrillers like Tom Clancy writes, it's not uncommon to find a third-person omniscient POV. If you're writing YA, you'll find lots of first-person POV.

In general, a tighter POV with less omniscience will force you to show more and not tell, and this will result in stronger writing.

Especially for inexperienced writers, lots of omniscience leads to weak and sloppy writing, and bloated novels with way too much explaining.

## MULTIPLE-POV STORIES

There is a temptation to write a novel with more than one POV—characters take turns telling the story in first-person, switching back and forth from chapter to chapter.

*Gone Girl* by Gillian Flynn is one of the best examples of this type of book. The narrative switches each chapter between the husband's and the wife's first-person POV. Obviously it can be done well, and we've seen a few breakout examples of this type of technique. Today, lots of people are trying to replicate those results…largely without success.

It is my strong recommendation that you not attempt this until you first master a single POV story.

A multiple-POV story is extremely difficult to pull off well. It makes your storytelling process much more complicated. It is the ruin of many first-time novelists.

I love it when stories do it well. But in my experience as a developmental editor, I can tell you that most first-time novelists end up with very poor projects when they try to do this. It's hard enough to pull off one well-developed voice and one well-developed storyline, let alone two or more.

I've seen books that include as many as five different first-person POVs. What I've learned from surveying readers is that many will begin to skip some of the POVs. They'll just thumb right past the chapters because they're only emotionally invested in one or two of the POV characters.

It's hard enough to get your reader to care about any more than the seven major character archetypes we've discussed. Can we really expect our reader to keep track of multiple sets of those characters?

Until you've mastered writing stories from one POV, I most strongly recommend that you do not embark on a multi-POV story. Keep it simple and constrain yourself to one point of view.

## CHOOSING A NARRATOR

Less is more when it comes to omniscience. Keeping your narrator's perspective tight will force you to write great *showing* prose.

After all, that's how we experience the real world. I don't know what anyone else is thinking (ask my wife). The further you travel from that natural human experience, the higher your reader's expectations will be for your execution.

Readers like to participate in the discovery process. They want to be fed little bits of information that they have to piece together. Having all the conclusions delivered to the page is boring. A limited narrator forces you to feed the reader data that he will assemble on his own, and that's a lot more fun and stimulating.

Before you begin writing, think carefully about who your narrator is and the voice you're trying to achieve. This simple step will increase the consistency of your writing and dramatically enhance your reader engagement.

# 18

# THE WORK

THE TRUTH that no one talks about: writing is work.

Yes, we can enjoy it. Yes, it can be inspired. But nonetheless, if we are to finish projects of any real magnitude, we have to come to terms with the work of it.

It's very difficult to stay inspired for 50,000+ words. For every finished project, a time comes when you have to push through and choose to do the work. By carefully conceptualizing and then execut-ing the project, you'll guarantee that when it starts to feel like work, you'll push through the Valley of the Shadow of Death and complete a great manuscript.

The Novel Matrix makes the work of writing predictable. Rather than operating in some sort of nebulous, open-ended work agreement, it turns the work of writing a novel into a predictable process. As you gain experience in the process, you'll be able to predict exactly how many hours you need to finish a project.

Today, there are a specific number of tasks standing between you and a finished novel manuscript. If you commit yourself to make a plan, then every time you complete a task there's one less task to be done.

These tasks fall into three major steps:

**Step 1:** Develop a complete Novel Matrix plan with scene list.
**Step 2:** Write the scenes.
**Step 3:** Revise your manuscript.

## STEP ONE: DEVELOP A COMPLETE NOVEL MATRIX PLAN

Don't skimp on the plan. The Novel Matrix only works if you take the time to apply it.

DOWNLOAD FULL-SIZE WORKSHEETS

FREE RESOURCES AT NOVELMATRIX.COM

Print the worksheets and fill them out. No matter how excited you are about the idea, don't allow yourself to move forward until you've completely conceptualized the story. You will thank yourself later.

Validate the plan using the tips provided in Chapter 14.

Develop a complete scene list, making sure that every component of your plan is represented and appropriately maintained. Not every element of the plan will get equal coverage in your novel.

Depending on your genre, you may choose to emphasize and give more scenes to either the internal or external conflict. Some secondary characters will also get more representation than others. That's okay. However, every element should be represented and maintained, at least periodically, through the manuscript.

### THE TEST DRIVE

When I mentor writers one-on-one, I do make an allowance to test drive the story. At any point in the planning and development process, you can write up to 3,000 words of the story.

This exercise may help you "see" the protagonist for the first time, to understand the universe of the story, or to get a feel for the narrative voice. That may help you fill in any remaining unassigned elements of the plan.

You may also find that you completely hate the idea! That is also a successful outcome. It's better to spend a couple of hours to find that out now, so that you can choose a different idea. That's better than floundering 20,000 words in.

Don't get carried away and soar past the 3,000 words. It may feel good, but you'll be glad that you stopped and charted a course first.

You can use this "test drive" exercise at any point—perhaps while you're just toying with the idea, or when you've hit a wall with certain elements. Your brain is good at story, give it a chance to play, and you'll work it out.

## Do the Work of the Plan

Developing a plan takes time. You probably can't do it in one session. You may need to ruminate and adjust for a couple of weeks even. Think about it while you drive your car and do the dishes. That's the work of conceptualizing a story. Within reason, it's not procrastination.

When I teach the Novel Matrix to groups, I usually develop a brand new story plan with them on the spot. I have tons of practice doing this, so I can usually make a new plan in about an hour. But I can assure you, it's not yet a good plan. Before I would act on any of those plans, I'd let it simmer for at least a week, tweaking the ideas until it feels just right. You may find it's reasonable to spend four to ten hours on a plan before you fully commit to it.

When the tweaking is complete, your plan is done.

**Once you finalize your plan, you're committing to complete that plan.** As you write, there will be times when you feel uncertain, insecure, or bored with your project. That doesn't mean it was a bad plan. You made a good plan. Fully commit to your plan so that you can push through those feelings when they rear their heads.

You may make changes after the plan is finalized. The plan is wet cement. As you write, you may discover that you need a scene that you hadn't considered, an element doesn't seem important anymore and needs to be removed, or a plot device won't work like you thought it would. You may make adjustments in that situation, but you shouldn't make a complete overhaul.

## STEP TWO: WRITE THE SCENES

Write the scenes in any order you choose.

In writing, *drafting* is the process of nailing down a first draft. You're not trying to craft a perfect book, you're just adding flesh to your scene list to write a complete story.

It usually makes sense to work through your plan from beginning to end, one scene at a time. However, one of the real assets of the Novel Matrix is that it positions you to write any scene in the book at any time. If you're inspired to write a particular scene, go ahead and do it. You don't have to wait until you get there. Jump around as much as you want.

If you're in the shower and you think of the perfect dialogue for a scene in act two, go ahead and fill it in. Maybe that gets the mojo working and you pound out the whole scene, maybe it just means that you drop a few lines in. It doesn't matter.

Perhaps you're sitting in traffic one day, and it's the perfect inspiration for the scene in which your protagonist is stuck in traffic. Go ahead and write that scene when you're inspired. No need to try to take notes for later, just do it right now.

Whenever you sit down, write the scenes that you're most excited to write. If you lack inspiration, simply write the next scene in order on your plan. This strategy will maximize your energy by allowing you to make the best use of your natural inspiration, while giving you a specific task to do when you sit down and don't feel the juice.

Sometimes you may plan a writing session and find that you're just out of gas. That's okay, just pick a scene and start filling in bullet points. Perhaps you can list some specific actions you know the protagonist will need to take, or maybe you know a few lines of dialogue—whatever it is, just fill out what you know.

Continue to move through the manuscript, developing the scenes with whatever details you know. At the very least, you'll continue to develop the plan, but I wouldn't be surprised if before long one of those bullet points turns into a full sentence, which turns into a paragraph, which turns into a scene.

As you write, you may realize that you need to add scenes that weren't part of your original plan. That's perfectly okay. The plan is wet cement. It's firm, but it's not set in stone.

It's common to be working on something in the third act and realize that you needed to introduce an element in the first act to justify it. For instance, maybe you have a clever idea for how the protagonist will solve the problem in the Near Miss, but in order to prevent *deus ex machina*, you need to inject a scene into the first act that introduces the fact that the protagonist is an oragami master. Go ahead and add that scene, or if possible, add that element to an existing scene.

## ALWAYS CREATE NEW MATERIAL

Whatever you do, when you're in this drafting step, always create new material. Resist the urge to read and revise what you already have. Drafting is a specific exercise. The goal is not to be perfect, the goal is to be done.

When you complete the full draft, you're going to see your own story for the first time. All kinds of light bulbs are going to go off in your mind. You will understand things about the story you couldn't fathom before you had written it all down. You will see connections and themes and foreshadowing that happened organically.

Until that happens, you don't yet have the best information to begin revising.

When you complete the first draft, you'll understand your own story for the first time.

Revising during drafting will only waste time—you'll just be spinning your wheels. You may spend hours revising a scene until it's beautiful, only to find that ultimately you cut the scene all together. Why not wait until you can see the whole story, and then invest in your revisions where you know they'll count?

You may make a reasonable exception to this rule for corrections.

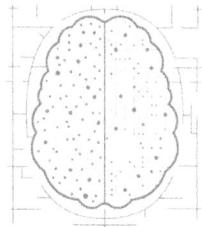

For instance, if in writing a new scene you realize that the sidekick's hair needs to be blonde for some reason, you can go back to the previous scenes and quickly make that change while it's top of mind. But don't get bogged down and begin revising large sections, just make the factual corrections and then move back to creating new material.

If you focus on drafting, it's very reasonable to draft at a rate of 1,000 words per hour. Make that your target. Focus on adding new content every session. If you can do this, you will have a complete draft of the story you intended to tell in less than 100 hours of writing.

## STEP THREE: REVISE

"The first draft is just you telling yourself the story."
Terry Pratchett

Complete the draft before you even think about revising. After you see the whole story on the page, you're going to understand it differently and more deeply than ever before. For the first time, you'll really get it. Armed with the whole story, beginning to end, you'll be able to accurately see what needs to be revised.

See the whole story first. Then make any big-picture structural revisions you need. After that's complete, dive into the fine details and revise the writing.

The Novel Matrix changes the revision game in one critical way: you can measure the novel you wrote against the novel you intended to write. You can ask a super important question, "Did I write the novel I set out to write?"

If you wrote a manuscript without a plan, how could you ever answer that question?

Since you made a plan and you used that plan, chances are extremely high that the answer is "yes!" The manuscript may not be great yet, it certainly won't be perfect, but at least you know it's in the right ballpark.

Maybe you've heard writers say things like this: originally my manuscript was a murder mystery about an English detective tracking down a jewel thief, but then I kept the sidekick and revised it into more of a coming-of-age romance about a young jewel thief, but then in my third draft I made it a coming-of-age zombie steampunk story about a young woman who wants to escape from her tyrant uncle.

I made that example up, but it is not an exaggeration. Amateur writers without guidance will fundamentally turn their manuscripts upside down with each revision.

If you dramatically change the premise of the story in revisions, then it wasn't a first draft at all, it was just an elaborate brainstorming exercise.

This often happens because the writer can tell the manuscript really isn't hitting the mark, but they have no idea why. Without any clues, the answer is *change everything*.

Fortunately, you have the answer! The Novel Matrix. The solution isn't to take another shot in the dark and change everything. The solution is to identify the elements that are missing, and then include them.

If something doesn't feel right in the story, then what's missing? What's underdeveloped? What's extra or overdeveloped? Compare your story to what you now know about the universe, the plot structure, the conflicts, and the character archetypes. What's not matching up well?

You may change the premise a little bit in revisions. For instance, after telling the story, you may see that the internal conflict had a lot more juice than you anticipated and became the driving idea as the story took shape. Totally normal. So your one-sentence premise may change from, "A man takes up arms with the rebels to drive back the invaders that killed his family," to, "A man overcomes his devastating personal loss to find new purpose, joining the rebellion's cause and winning a critical battle." But that's a change in nuance and emphasis, not a dramatic change in premise.

We have to revise from a place of "I told the story I wanted to tell, now it's time to solve the problems." We had a plan, we used the plan, now let's find the bugs and work it out. We're maintaining the same essential story, we're just improving it. That's what revisions are.

Just like writing, revision is a finite process. It doesn't have to go on for some unpredictable amount of time. There are logical steps to complete.

I designed a process called "The 4-step Novel Revision Plan." You can get it for free by joining The Company at Writers.Company.

THE 4-STEP
NOVEL REVISION PLAN:

FREE RESOURCE AT
WRITERS.COMPANY

This four-step process provides a logical order to revisions, and constrains the process to a predictable amount of work. Follow the process and then you get to call it done!

Nothing is perfect. Even Michaelangelo's *David* probably has room for improvement. He probably could have spent his whole life making it a little better and a little better. Thank God that at some point he said "good enough" and moved on to many other wonderful projects.

Even when your revisions are done, the manuscript doesn't have to be perfect yet. If you move forward with publication, you will revisit it with professional help and make it even better.

This is the work of the Novel Matrix—the process of applying all of that theory to execute a great novel-length story.

One universe, three acts, five conflicts, seven characters—to turn a nobody into somebody who does impossible things.

Confidence is a game changer, and that's what the Novel Matrix gives you. When you get discouraged or tired of your idea, you can fall back on your Novel Matrix plan. You can look it over and know in your heart that you're investing your time wisely. This work will produce something worthwhile.

There's no guarantee of wild success, but you're behaving in a prudent manner that is likely to produce the best possible outcome. And that's the best any of us can do.

When discouragement, boredom, or seasonal changes threaten the project, your plan is a powerful weapon.

# 19

# CONCLUSION

ONE UNIVERSE. Three acts. Five conflicts. Seven characters.

One protagonist accomplishing a seemingly impossible thing.

These elements will help you craft a story that reflects your reader's intuitive understanding of stories and how the world works. If you include these elements, your novel will be robust enough to justify six hours of someone's attention. Your reader will leave the story feeling resolved and thoughtful.

With this method, you can develop a story that "works" before you put hours and hours into the writing. The days of writing yourself into a hole are done. The days of getting to 50,000 words, but realizing that it's a flatline of a story are over.

With the Novel Matrix, you're prepared to do the work of a writer in a logical manner. You can start producing great stories on a regular basis and, more importantly, you can begin influencing readers about the things that are important to you.

Just like a cake has certain elements or it's just not a cake, a novel has particular elements or it's just not a novel. This isn't a formula, we've simply described what the art form we call a "novel" is. You can apply these concepts to virtually any project, adding your own unique flavors, and you will produce a one-of-a-kind, masterful piece of art. The possibilities are endless.

Knowing the ingredients doesn't stifle your creativity. On the contrary, it allows you to bring your creations to life!

The majority of award-winning and bestselling books of the past 100 years conform to this model, whether the author intended to or just got lucky.

When you make a plan based on a working understanding of these concepts, you can move forward with confidence. The novel project that used to seem mysterious and unquantifiable is now nailed down in a broad outline.

There is a finite amount of work standing between you and a finished novel manuscript. Not just 50,000 words of drivel, but an actual novel with all of the critical components in place. For most authors using this plan, your first draft is less than 100 hours of work away. 100 hours! You can do that.

When you're done with that draft, revisions will be different than you've ever experienced before. You haven't written a random story. You've written the story that you intended. It's not perfect yet, you'll see all kinds of new connections and ways to take it to the next level after the story is on the page. Nonetheless, you can operate with the confidence that the story is essentially complete. Never again will you completely overhaul a finished draft to change the genre and the premise. Instead, your revisions will usher the story you planned to completion.

For most writers, this is a completely new way of looking at stories. In school, teachers tell us to focus on "themes" in literature. This is a mechanism that forces young readers to actually read a book, internalize it, and have some vaguely original thought about it. From an academic perspective, that's a big win, and I mean that. However, that conversation doesn't really help us to understand how and why stories work.

As writers, all of our talk about "themes" is premature until we master these fundamentals.

As you move forward consuming stories—reading books, watching movies, chatting with friends—incorporate the Novel Matrix elements into the way you think and talk about stories.

What made the story work? In what ways did it use the established conventions of story that we've discussed here? When a story breaks the rules, was it a mistake that left you unfulfilled, or was it an intentional choice to create dissonance or draw your attention to something? When you feel an emotion, good or bad, why did you feel it? What specifically did the author do to achieve that emotional response?

If you consume a story that leaves you feeling underwhelmed, can you trace the source of that feeling back to one of the Novel Matrix concepts? Is something missing?

Perhaps in the future, middle and high school literature teachers will begin discussing stories in terms of mechanics. I think it would positively change the way many students interact with literature.

You can begin to train your brain to perceive stories in terms of structure and mechanics right away. It will take some practice, but you'll probably never watch a movie the same way again. As a story mechanic, you'll be able to predict the events of almost any movie you watch. Within the first forty minutes, you'll be able to lean over to your friends and tell them exactly what's going to happen and when. Plus, you'll always know when to go to the bathroom so you won't miss anything cool.

The Novel Matrix is the most important tool in the novelist's belt. Without an understanding of what a novel is, it really doesn't matter how amazing your prose are, the depth of your character development, or how real and compelling your dialogue is. The story will fall flat.

If we're being honest, there are all kinds of successful books in which the writing really isn't that great. But those books hit the story marks. In the real market, great story structure with mediocre writing beats amazing writing with zero story sense every single day. It's not even really a contest.

The Novel Matrix isn't a magic bullet. However, if you can marry this tool with exceptional prose craft, you'll be in a position to achieve real results with your work.

When I worked as a developmental editor, most manuscripts would require two complete rounds of revision. With the first revision, I would just help the writer improve his story structure. Once that was complete, then we would go through it again and work out the prose craft to make it sound good.

Now, when I work with authors who have applied the Novel Matrix, I often no longer have to do that first step. Nothing's perfect, so there might be some minor tweaks or opportunities for improvement, but their structure is sound. That means that we can focus all of our attention on fine-tuning the writing and making it sing.

After practicing the Novel Matrix and learning to consume stories all around you through these paradigms, you may grow to no longer need it. It's possible to train yourself to think in story, so that you intuitively begin to employ these ideas in your work.

Until that time comes, force yourself to commit to the system, to use it over and over again, proving it to yourself and ingraining story mechanics into the way you consume the stories around you. Take the time to fill out the worksheets again and again. After this method becomes your first nature, then you'll be in a position to intentionally deviate from it and manipulate it. It won't be by accident when it happens, it will be because you are a professional, you know exactly what you're doing, and you are achieving the effect you intended.

The Novel Matrix isn't a prescription, it's a description of what great literature does. I didn't invent it, I observed it. I've

Visit
NovelMatrix.com
for
· Downloadable
  Worksheets
· Video Courses
· Writing Craft Resources
· Support Community

helped hundreds of authors apply it and it works. These simple concepts turn a project that once seemed nebulous and impossible into a

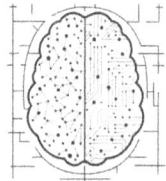

reasonable task that you can complete.

You now know what the great literary geniuses of old could only stumble upon.

There are important things that you need to talk about, important stories you need to tell. It is not dramatic to say that the fate of the world hangs in the balance.

You hold in your hands the power to change the world.

Time to write.

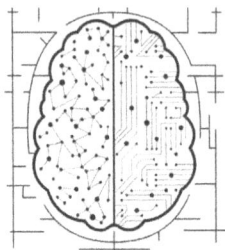

# FINAL NOTE

AS ONE FINAL PIECE OF ADVICE, find one system like the Novel Matrix and stick with it. Too much knowledge can be a bad thing. I'm not the only "expert" with a model that will make your writing work. I think the Novel Matrix is the best because it's the simplest method to understand, comprehensively relates all of the pieces together, and preserves your flexibility, (plus there's a universe of support available), but I'm biased. There are certainly other good ones out there. Pick one.

In my experience working the Novel Matrix with authors, the ones that get the most confused are the ones that start talking about "inciting incidents" and "midpoints" and "compelling trauma." There's a whole mess to be made trying to graft those ideas onto the Novel Matrix. Some people have read too many books on the subject. You can't hammer screws, and you can't screw nails. Pick one system and stick to it.

# ACKNOWLEDGMENTS

I think it's amazing that I get to write books and help other people write books for a living, and I thank God for that. I'm not in any way qualified to tell another human being how to do anything, except by the doors God has opened for me, the talents he planted in me, and the authority he lends me as a servant of his son Jesus.

Many people have contributed to the Novel Matrix over the years. I especially want to thank (and apologize to, haha) all of those students who took early versions of my novel writing courses so many years ago. Watching you write and hearing your feedback has been invaluable in developing this method to what it has become today.

I want to thank my students and apprentices at The Company who helped with the development, design, and production of this work, most notably Alli Prince, Thirzah, and Rebekah Olson. Thank you each for believing in the work that we do together, and contributing your time and skills to it.

Thank you to Molly Glucklich and all of my early readers who helped us find and correct errors in the text.

Of course there are too many writers and filmmakers to list that have contributed to my understanding of story, but a special thank you to all of those that contributed to the example books and movies referenced in the Novel Matrix including John Steinbeck, Kurt Vonnegut, Donald Miller, and George Lucas. I wish we could talk about stories all day, because I surely would have included many more examples if I could.

Speaking of which, if you'd like to live in this world of writing with me, please check out The Company. I'm always looking for new apprentices to join us in Cambridge, Ohio, and there's also a variety of ways that we can hang out online.

And my biggest thank you to my wife Melissa, who is really good at saying "no" to my crazy ideas, but never stops pushing me and supporting me once she says, "yes."

Thanks for reading *The Novel Matrix*. I hope we can meet in real life sometime soon. If you use the Novel Matrix to write something, please tell me about it. I'd love to celebrate with you! You can always reach out to me via my website, BradPauquette.com.

# ABOUT BRAD PAUQUETTE

Brad has worked in the publishing industry since 2009. He is the editor of many books and anthologies, and a published author. As a publishing consultant and developmental editor, Brad has coached award-winning and *New York Times* bestselling authors to produce exceptional books and reach new audiences.

Brad and his wife, Melissa, have developed and sold multiple publishing imprints, and founded the Ohio Writers Association.

Brad lives in Cambridge, Ohio with his wife and six kids. Learn more about him at BradPauquette.com.

Brad is presently the director of The Company, a community of Christian writers on a mission to change the world. Every fall, Brad welcomes new apprentices to The Company's two-year writing and publishing training program. If you're ready to take your writing to the next level, learn more at Writers.Company.

# HELP OTHER WRITERS

I don't know if you've noticed, but there's a lot of bad advice out there about writing and publishing. Will you help people find the good stuff?

If you enjoyed *The Novel Matrix*, if it sparked something in you, then it's up to you to help other writers find this resource. In the marketplace of ideas, it's up to you to help this information rise above the junk.

Here are two important ways you can do that:

## 1. LEAVE A REVIEW

Your reviews help readers sift through all of the available resources. Please leave an honest review on Amazon, but you can also leave a review on Goodreads or wherever else you typically review books.

## 2. TELL A FRIEND

It's easy. "Jim, I just read this book that changed my perspective on writing. Will you check it out and tell me what you think?" See how easy that was?

If you're part of a writing group, you can even tell them about it. Contact me via my website, BradPauquette.com, and there's a good chance I can schedule a time to come visit. I'd love to meet your group and talk story!

Thanks for helping great books break out! We're changing the world together, you and me.

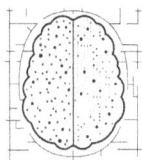

# BLANK NOVEL MATRIX WORKSHEETS

**Contents:**

One Universe Worksheet

Three Acts Worksheet

Five Conflicts Worksheet

Seven Characters Worksheet

Scene Plan

DOWNLOAD FULL-SIZE
WORKSHEETS

FREE RESOURCES AT
NOVELMATRIX.COM

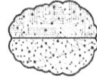

One Universe 🧠 the novel matrix

| ELEMENT | WHAT'S POSSIBLE? | WHAT'S NORMAL? |
|---|---|---|
| SOCIAL NORMS | | |
| MAGIC/SUPERNATURAL | | |
| PHYSICAL ACTIONS/ REACTIONS | | |
| ROMANCE/LOVE | | |

| SERENDIPITY | | |
|---|---|---|
| **TECHNOLOGY** | | |
| *(ADDITIONAL ELEMENT)* | | |
| *(ADDITIONAL ELEMENT)* | | |

Highlight items that have a direct bearing on the plot and premise of your story. Specifically develop these elements early in the manuscript.

# Three-Act Structure

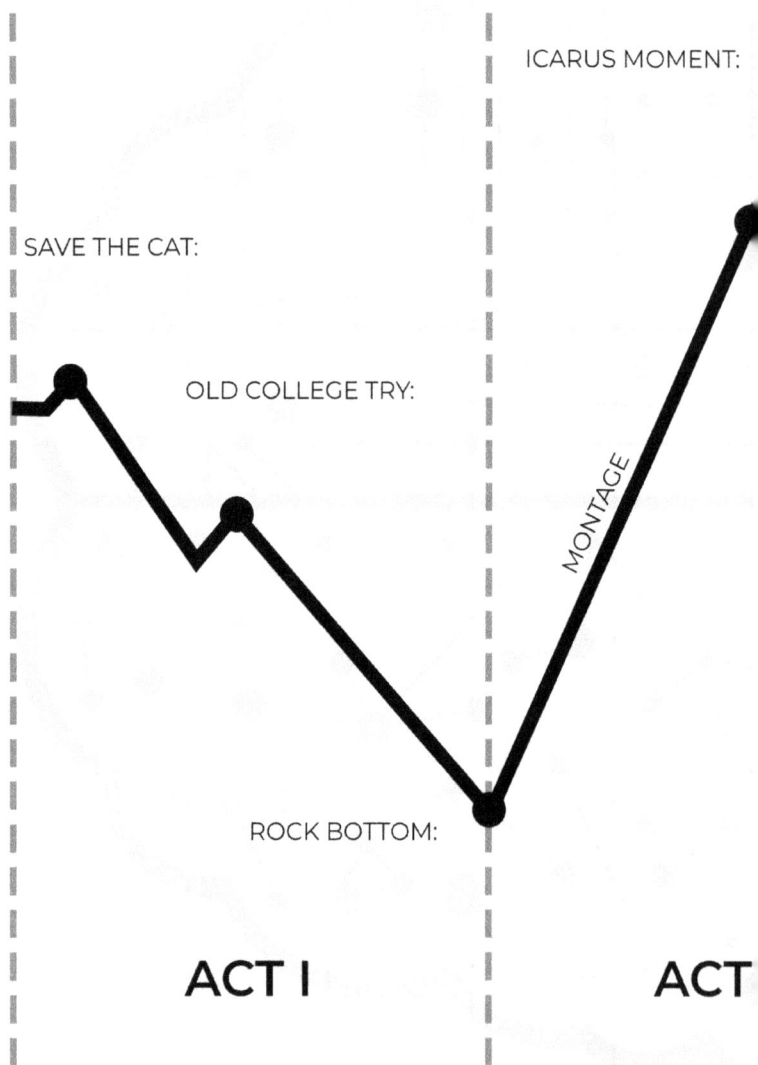

ICARUS MOMENT:

SAVE THE CAT:

OLD COLLEGE TRY:

MONTAGE

ROCK BOTTOM:

**ACT I**

**ACT**

How is the protagonist trapped
(without agency)?

# the novel matrix

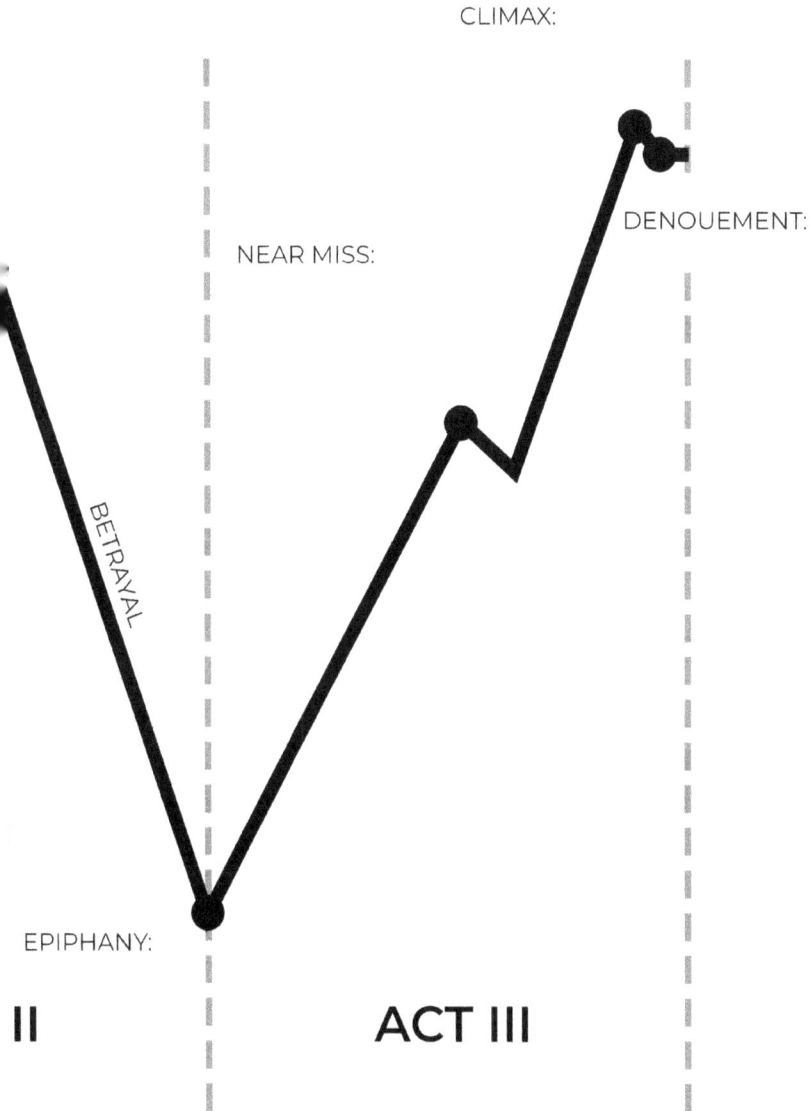

CLIMAX:

NEAR MISS:

DENOUEMENT:

BETRAYAL

EPIPHANY:

II

ACT III

What **Impossible Thing** will
the protagonist achieve?

# Five Conflicts

## Little World Conflicts

**INTERNAL**

*TWO INCOMPATIBLE THINGS
THE PROTAGONIST DESIRES*

**EXTERNAL**

*A DIRECT CONTEST WITH A
NAMEABLE ENTITY*

**PHILOSOPHICAL**

*TWO OPPOSING
WORLDVIEWS*

## Big World Conflicts

**INTERNAL**

X

**EXTERNAL**

*TWO PEOPLE GROUPS IN
CONFLICT*

**PHILOSOPHICAL**

*TWO IDEAS OF HOW THE
WORLD OUGHT TO BE*

Put a square around the **Driving Conflict**.

How will the LW external conflict manifest?
Are the protagonist and antagonist in
competition for the same thing,
or do they have mutually exclusive goals?

How will the LW internal conflict manifest?
What will happen that shows and
amplifies the problem in
the protagonist's heart?

Full-size printable worksheet available at
**NovelMatrix.com**

# Seven Characters

🧠 **the novel matrix**

| ARCHETYPE | FUNCTION | CHARACTER |
|---|---|---|
| GUIDE | 1. EXPLAINS THE UNIVERSE<br>2. ESTABLISHES THE PROTAGONIST'S MISSION | |
| SIDEKICK | 1. PROVIDES TOOLS, SKILLS, AND RESOURCES<br>2. ESTABLISHES LIKEABILITY | |
| FRENEMY | 1. INJECTS A VARIABLE INTO THE SCENE<br>2. MAY BE POS. OR NEG. | |
| OBJECT OF AFFECTION | 1. CATALYZES THE PROTAGONIST TO ACTION<br>2. IS NEVER HELPFUL | |
| ANTAGONIST | 1. DIRECTLY OPPOSES PROTAGONIST<br>2. OFTEN A VICTIM OF THE SYSTEM | |
| MEGA-ANTAGONIST | 1. REPRESENTS EVERYTHING WRONG WITH THE UNIVERSE<br>2. JUST PLAIN EVIL | |

|  | GUIDE | SIDEKICK | FRENEMY | OBJECT | ANTAGONIST | MEGA-A |
|---|---|---|---|---|---|---|
| GUIDE | | | ✓ | ✓ | | |
| SIDEKICK | | | | | | |
| FRENEMY | ✓ | | | | | |
| OBJECT | ✓ | | | | ✓ | |
| ANTAGONIST | | | ✓ | | | |
| MEGA-A | | | | | | |

**REASONABLE CHARACTER COMBOS**

Which two characters will embody the LW philosophical conflict?

[ ]

[ ]

Full-size printable worksheet available at
**NovelMatrix.com**

# SCENE PLAN

SCENE TITLE

ACT          SCENE #

SCENE DESCRIPTION

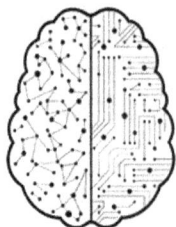

## VALIDATE SCENE

☐ MOTIVATE PLOT

☐ DEVELOP CHARACTER

☐ REINFORCE THEMES

MUST CHECK 2 OF 3

PURPOSE OF SCENE

PLOT POINTS DEVELOPED

CONFLICTS SERVICED

CHARACTERS DEVELOPED

STAKES RAISED

SUBPLOTS DEVELOPED

THEME OR VOICE

WHAT CHANGES IN THIS SCENE?

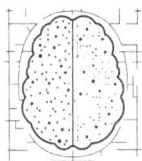

# *STAR WARS* NOVEL MATRIX WORKSHEETS

## Contents:

Find additional example plans at
**NovelMatrix.com**

229

# One Universe

## *Star Wars: Episode IV*

# the novel matrix

| ELEMENT | WHAT'S POSSIBLE? | WHAT'S NORMAL? |
|---------|------------------|----------------|
| SOCIAL NORMS | Social classes exist between members of the empire and regular members of society, as well as a royal class. Children speak freely with adults. | Common people expect to be mistreated by the empire. Strangers are not trusted. Discrimination between alien life forms common. Honor/duty/royalty is antiquated. |
| MAGIC/SUPERNATURAL | "The Force" is a seemingly supernatural phenomenon that gives telekenesis, telepathy, and unnatural strength. Must be gifted and practiced. | Most individuals know very little about "The Force" and do not use it. Most people live without ever experiencing supernatural forces. |
| PHYSICAL ACTIONS/ REACTIONS | When people fall from high things they break bones. Weapons cause bruising, bleeding, and amputation. Alien-life forms and robots follow same rules. | Good guys get injured, bad guys die. Good guys are good shots, bad guys are not. Death in combat is very commonplace. |
| ROMANCE/LOVE | Love is biological attraction. Relationships between men and women sometimes exhibit sexual attraction/tension. Dating/marriage not a factor. | If boys and girls are attracted to each other, they'll engage in flirtation or kissing, which is relatively meaningless. |

| | | |
|---|---|---|
| **SERENDIPITY** | Fate/destiny are driving forces in the universe. Destinies can be stopped or delayed, which is a source of both hope and fear. | Most people do not have a specific fate or destiny, and have little faith, knowledge, or understanding of destiny or mythology. |
| **TECHNOLOGY** | Spaceships and laser guns exist. Spaceships capable of traveling faster than light. Some computers, but most technology is mechanical with buttons and levers. | Most people have wide access to technology, including weapons. Interstellar travel is common. Broken technology can typically be easily repaired. |
| *(ADDITIONAL ELEMENT)* | | |
| *(ADDITIONAL ELEMENT)* | | |

Highlight items that have a direct bearing on the plot and premise of your story. Specifically develop these elements early in the manuscript.

# Three-Act Structure
## *Star Wars: Episode IV - A New Hope*

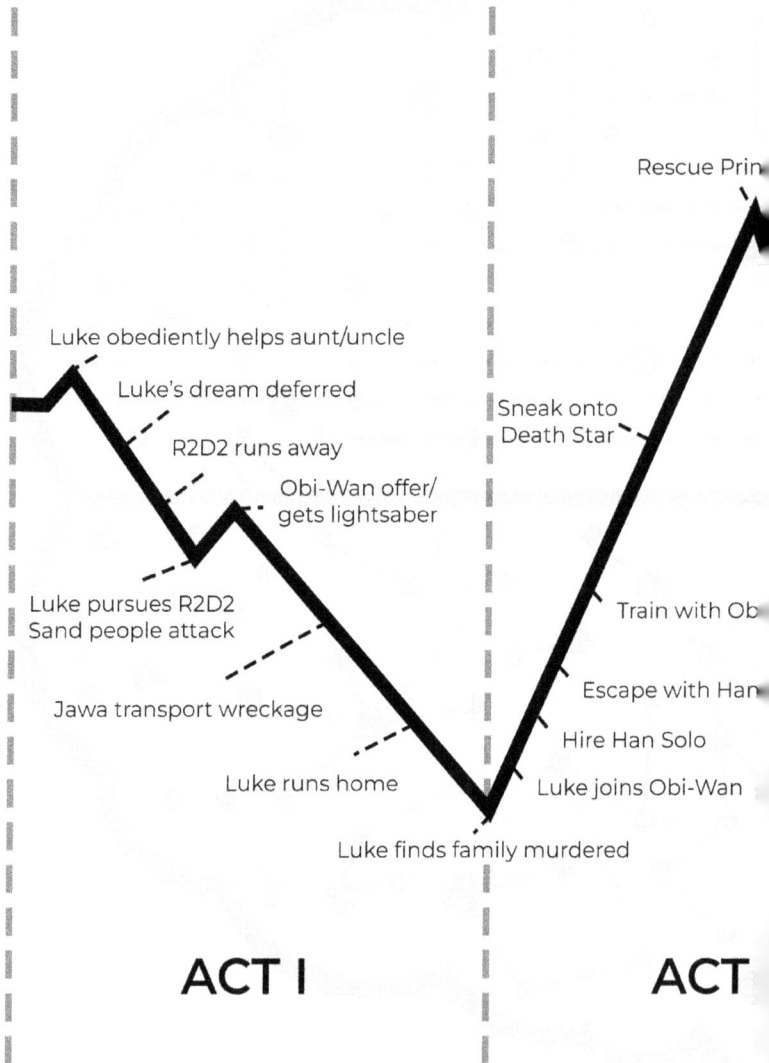

Rescue Prin

Luke obediently helps aunt/uncle

Luke's dream deferred

Sneak onto
Death Star

R2D2 runs away

Obi-Wan offer/
gets lightsaber

Luke pursues R2D2
Sand people attack

Train with Ob

Escape with Han

Jawa transport wreckage

Hire Han Solo

Luke runs home

Luke joins Obi-Wan

Luke finds family murdered

**ACT I**

**ACT**

How is the protagonist trapped
(without agency)?

His age, naivete, and family obligations

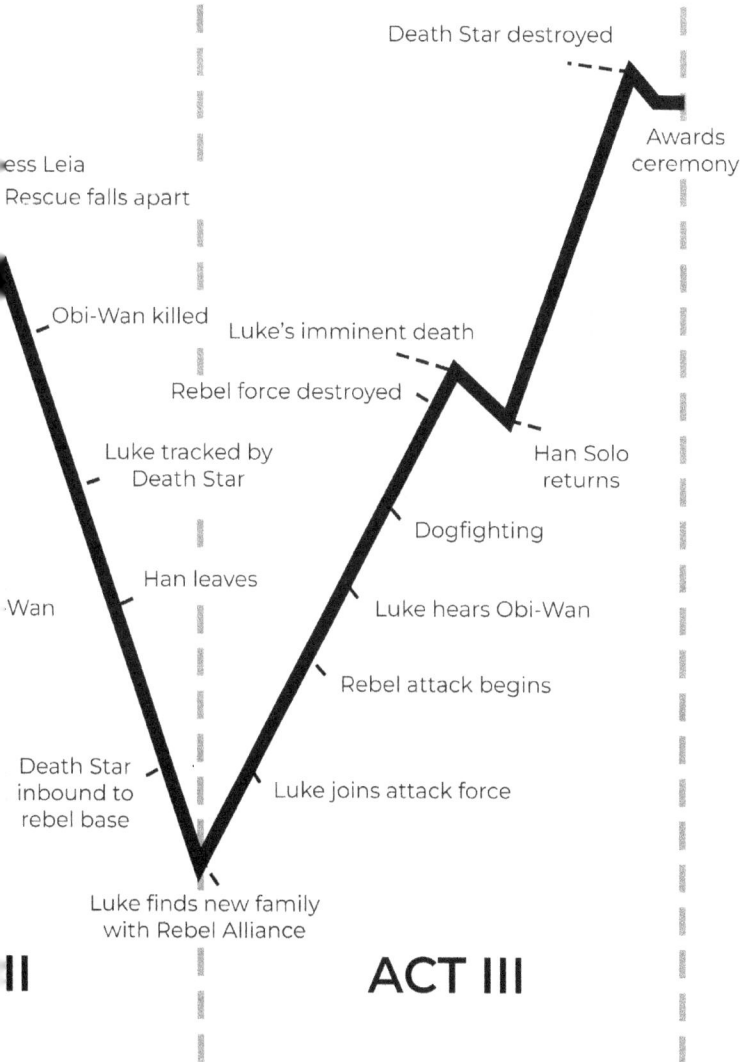

the novel matrix

Death Star destroyed

Awards
ceremony

ess Leia
Rescue falls apart

Obi-Wan killed

Luke's imminent death

Rebel force destroyed

Luke tracked by
Death Star

Han Solo
returns

Dogfighting

Han leaves

Luke hears Obi-Wan

-Wan

Rebel attack begins

Death Star
inbound to
rebel base

Luke joins attack force

Luke finds new family
with Rebel Alliance

II

ACT III

What **Impossible Thing** will
the protagonist achieve?

Destroy the Death Star

# Five Conflicts

*Star Wars: Episode IV*

🧠 **the novel matrix**

## Little World Conflicts

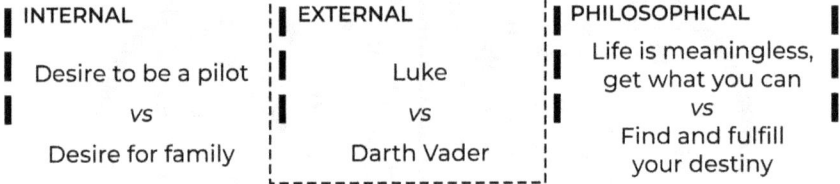

| **INTERNAL** | **EXTERNAL** | **PHILOSOPHICAL** |
|---|---|---|
| Desire to be a pilot | Luke | Life is meaningless, get what you can |
| vs | vs | vs |
| Desire for family | Darth Vader | Find and fulfill your destiny |

## Big World Conflicts

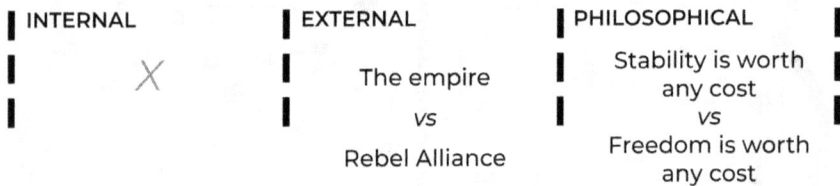

| **INTERNAL** | **EXTERNAL** | **PHILOSOPHICAL** |
|---|---|---|
| X | The empire | Stability is worth any cost |
|  | vs | vs |
|  | Rebel Alliance | Freedom is worth any cost |

Put a square around the **Driving Conflict**.

---

**How will the LW external conflict manifest?**
Are the protagonist and antagonist in competition for the same thing, or do they have mutually exclusive goals?

> Luke and Darth Vader will battle over the Death Star.

**How will the LW internal conflict manifest?**
What will happen that shows and amplifies the problem in the protagonist's heart?

> Luke will lose his family, but then find a new family in the Rebel Alliance. This "new family" will support his dream.

# Seven Characters
*Star Wars: Episode IV*

## the novel matrix

| ARCHETYPE | FUNCTION | CHARACTER |
|---|---|---|
| GUIDE | 1. EXPLAINS THE UNIVERSE<br>2. ESTABLISHES THE PROTAGONIST'S MISSION | Obi-Wan Kenobi |
| SIDEKICK | 1. PROVIDES TOOLS, SKILLS, AND RESOURCES<br>2. ESTABLISHES LIKEABILITY | R2D2 |
| FRENEMY | 1. INJECTS A VARIABLE INTO THE SCENE<br>2. MAY BE POS. OR NEG. | Han Solo |
| OBJECT OF AFFECTION | 1. CATALYZES THE PROTAGONIST TO ACTION<br>2. IS NEVER HELPFUL | Princess Leia |
| ANTAGONIST | 1. DIRECTLY OPPOSES PROTAGONIST<br>2. OFTEN A VICTIM OF THE SYSTEM | Darth Vader |
| MEGA-ANTAGONIST | 1. REPRESENTS EVERYTHING WRONG WITH THE UNIVERSE<br>2. JUST PLAIN EVIL | The Emperor |

| | GUIDE | SIDEKICK | FRENEMY | OBJECT | ANTAGONIST | MEGA-A |
|---|---|---|---|---|---|---|
| GUIDE | | | ✓ | ✓ | | |
| SIDEKICK | | | | | | |
| FRENEMY | ✓ | | | | | |
| OBJECT | ✓ | | | ✓ | | |
| ANTAGONIST | | | ✓ | | | |
| MEGA-A | | | | | | |

REASONABLE CHARACTER COMBOS

Which two characters will embody the LW philosophical conflict?

Obi-Wan Kenobi

Han Solo

## Notes on
# Star Wars: Episode IV

*Star Wars* is a classic example of the three-act structure. The storytelling may be simplistic, but for generations now, the story just works.

One of the most notable aspects of *Star Wars* is the use of combination characters. Two of the secondary characters have a tag-along buddy that makes the character more fun. What's even more interesting is that in each of these combinations, one of the characters is effectively mute!

While R2D2 is the sidekick, his buddy C3PO is never far away. R2D2 does all of the things the sidekick needs to do, but he can't talk. C3PO provides comic relief and acts as a mouthpiece for R2D2.

Conversely, Han Solo is our frenemy. He's joined by Chewbacca, who does not talk.

Importantly, neither Chewbacca nor C3PO take any real action apart from their functional character. This prevents the character list from becoming unnecessarily bloated. These two tag-along characters only exist as an extension of the functionary character.

While you can write an incredibly complex story using the Novel Matrix method, *Star Wars* is proof that simple stories can do the trick!

*Star Wars* was written by George Lucas.

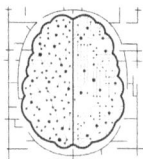

# *THE GODFATHER* NOVEL MATRIX WORKSHEETS

**Contents:**

*The Godfather* One Universe

*The Godfather* Three Acts

*The Godfather* Five Conflicts Worksheet

*The Godfather* Seven Characters Worksheet

Find additional example plans at
**NovelMatrix.com**

# the novel matrix

## One Universe
### The Godfather

| ELEMENT | WHAT'S POSSIBLE? | WHAT'S NORMAL? |
|---|---|---|
| SOCIAL NORMS | A class system exists between members of the crime family, employes of the crime family, and non-members. | Members of each class persistently mistreat members of lower classes. It's normal to carry weapons and engage in violence. |
| MAGIC/SUPERNATURAL | There is no magical or supernatural bearing on the story. | Most characters, even criminals, are nominally Catholic. They engage in religious ceremony but show no evidence of any real faith walk. |
| PHYSICAL ACTIONS/ REACTIONS | A good punch can cause significant damage. Bullets to the head cause death, bullets to the body may be survivable. | While characters are prone to violent rhetoric, they try to avoid violent confrontation whenever possible due to the very high risk of serious injury or death. |
| ROMANCE/LOVE | Love is biological attraction. There is no "true love." Love is a pragmatic matter. Kissing or other physical expressions are usually not meaningful. | Some characters have regard for the sanctity of marriage, others do not. Privacy is usually respected. |

| | | |
|---|---|---|
| **SERENDIPITY** | Destiny is not a driving force of the universe. Actions, reactions, and the future are governed by pragmatism and duty to family. | Characters succeed (or fail) due to their own cunning. The most strategic characters succeed on their own merits. |
| **TECHNOLOGY** | Set in the late 1940s, the technology is consistent with the actual technology of the time period. | Telephones/communication is limited to physical houses/offices. Guns are carried by employees, but not by family or non-criminals. Access to cars is common but not universal. |
| **POLICE** | Almost all police and government officials are susceptible to corruption. | Criminals do not fear police. Criminals are policed by the code of ethics (honor) of the organized crime families. |
| *(ADDITIONAL ELEMENT)* | | |
| *(ADDITIONAL ELEMENT)* | | |

Highlight items that have a direct bearing on the plot and premise of your story. Specifically develop these elements early in the manuscript.

# Three-Act Structure
*The Godfather*

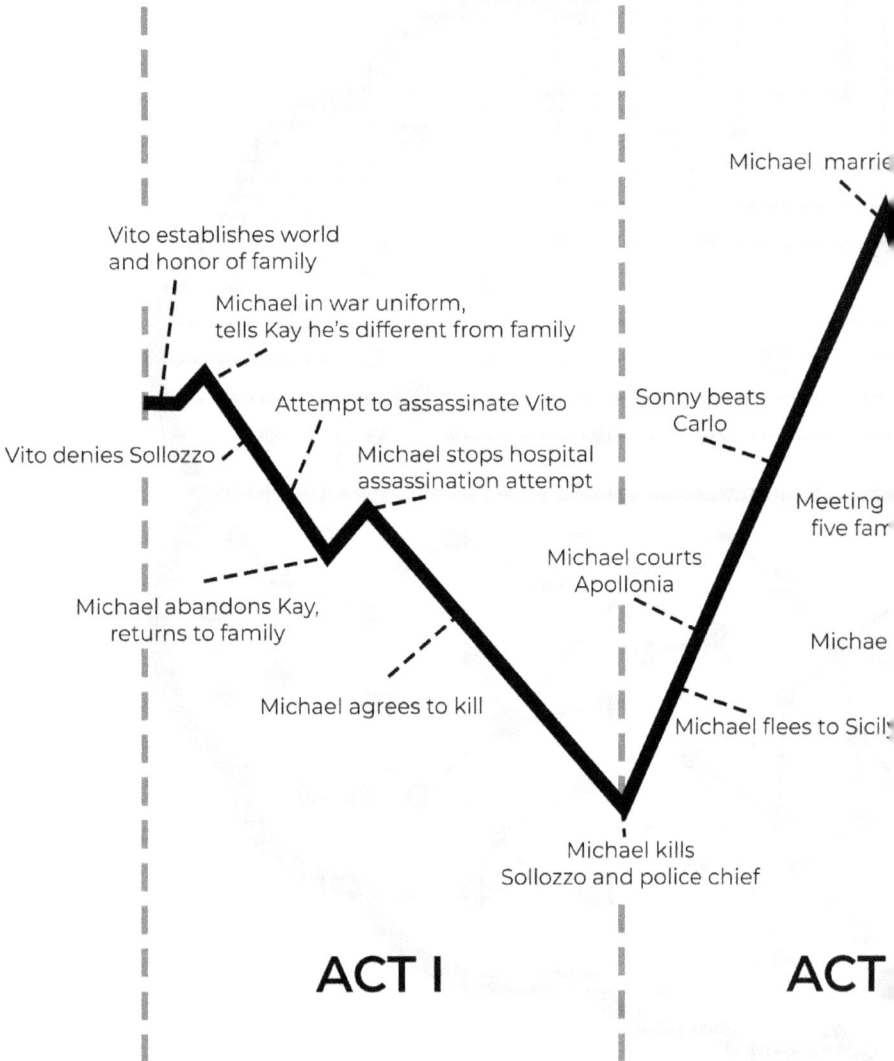

Michael marrie

Vito establishes world
and honor of family

Michael in war uniform,
tells Kay he's different from family

Attempt to assassinate Vito

Sonny beats
Carlo

Vito denies Sollozzo

Michael stops hospital
assassination attempt

Meeting
five fam

Michael courts
Apollonia

Michael abandons Kay,
returns to family

Michae

Michael agrees to kill

Michael flees to Sicily

Michael kills
Sollozzo and police chief

## ACT I

## ACT

How is the protagonist trapped
(without agency)?

Michael is caught between two worlds
and doesn't fit in either one.

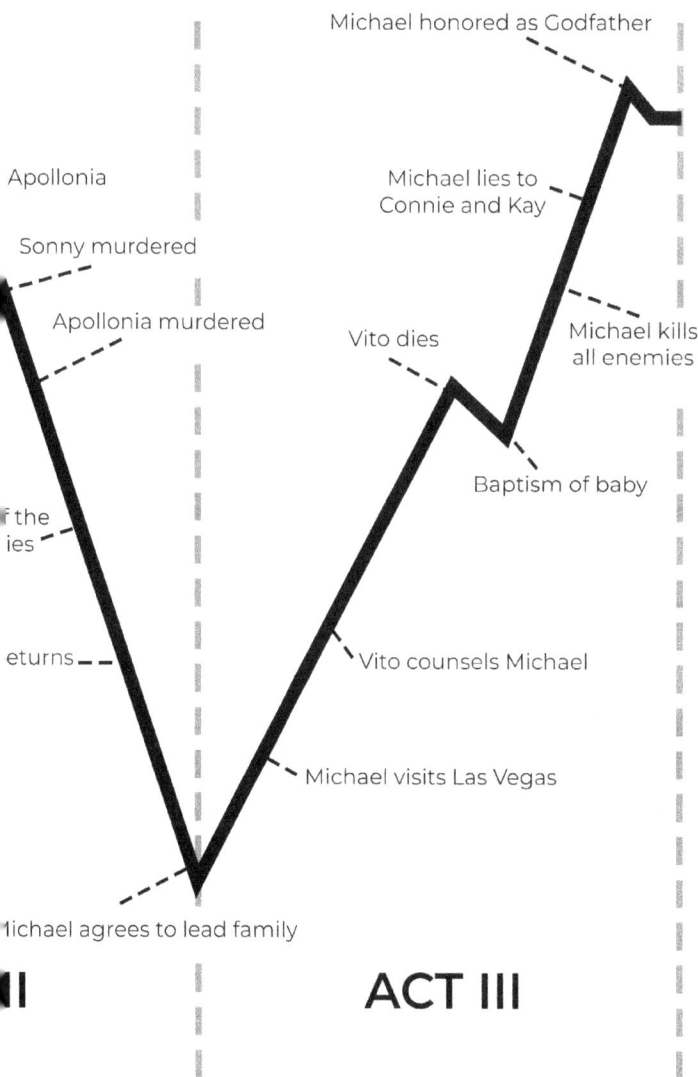

![brain icon] **the novel matrix**

Michael honored as Godfather

Apollonia

Sonny murdered

Apollonia murdered

Michael lies to
Connie and Kay

Vito dies

Michael kills
all enemies

the
ies

Baptism of baby

eturns

Vito counsels Michael

Michael visits Las Vegas

Michael agrees to lead family

**II**

**ACT III**

What **Impossible Thing** will
the protagonist achieve?

Become the most ruthless crime boss ever.

# Five Conflicts

*The Godfather*

**the novel matrix**

## Little World Conflicts

**INTERNAL**

Live straight life

*vs*

Fulfill duty to family

**EXTERNAL**

Michael

*vs*

Sollozzo

**PHILOSOPHICAL**

Criminals must have honor

*vs*

Violence is the path to power

## Big World Conflicts

**INTERNAL**

X

**EXTERNAL**

The Corleone Family

*vs*

The other four families

**PHILOSOPHICAL**

Drug business is not worth the cost

*vs*

Drugs are the path forward

Put a square around the **Driving Conflict**.

---

How will the LW external conflict manifest?
Are the protagonist and antagonist in competition for the same thing, or do they have mutually exclusive goals?

> Michael, as a proxy of his father Vito, will contend with Sollozzo over including drugs in the family crime business.

How will the LW internal conflict manifest?
What will happen that shows and amplifies the problem in the protagonist's heart?

> The story will contrast Michael's romantic storyline with the series of events pulling him into a do-or-die moment for the family.

# Seven Characters

*The Godfather*

🧠 **the novel matrix**

| ARCHETYPE | FUNCTION | CHARACTER |
|---|---|---|
| GUIDE | 1. EXPLAINS THE UNIVERSE<br>2. ESTABLISHES THE PROTAGONIST'S MISSION | Vito Corleone |
| SIDEKICK | 1. PROVIDES TOOLS, SKILLS, AND RESOURCES<br>2. ESTABLISHES LIKEABILITY | Tom Hagen |
| FRENEMY | 1. INJECTS A VARIABLE INTO THE SCENE<br>2. MAY BE POS. OR NEG. | Sonny Corleone |
| OBJECT OF AFFECTION | 1. CATALYZES THE PROTAGONIST TO ACTION<br>2. IS NEVER HELPFUL | Vito Corleone |
| ANTAGONIST | 1. DIRECTLY OPPOSES PROTAGONIST<br>2. OFTEN A VICTIM OF THE SYSTEM | Sollozzo |
| MEGA-ANTAGONIST | 1. REPRESENTS EVERYTHING WRONG WITH THE UNIVERSE<br>2. JUST PLAIN EVIL | Barzini |

|  | GUIDE | SIDEKICK | FRENEMY | OBJECT | ANTAGONIST | MEGA-A |
|---|---|---|---|---|---|---|
| GUIDE |  |  | ✓ | ✓ |  |  |
| SIDEKICK |  |  |  |  |  |  |
| FRENEMY | ✓ |  |  |  |  |  |
| OBJECT | ✓ |  |  |  | ✓ |  |
| ANTAGONIST |  |  | ✓ |  |  |  |
| MEGA-A |  |  |  |  |  |  |

**REASONABLE CHARACTER COMBOS**

Which two characters will embody the LW philosophical conflict?

> Vito Corleone

> Sonny Corleone

## Notes on
# The Godfather

While we might typically associate a crime movie with the external conflict, *The Godfather* is actually driven by Michael's internal conflict. We watch as Michael resolves how he'll follow in his father's footsteps.

This conflict relates very closely to the Little World Philosophical conflict, and the interplay between the two conflicts creates irony. Ultimately, while Michael follows in his father's footsteps, he abandons his father's ethics.

We see a combination character in Vito Corleone, who performs the function of Guide and Object of Affection.

As the Guide, Vito explains the rules of the universe, including the code of ethics, to the viewer/reader. However, as the Object of Affection, he's also the character who can draw Michael into things he shouldn't be doing. Michael takes his first step into the crime family when he protects Vito from the second assassination attempt in the "Old College Try." He tells his father, "I'm with you now," and begins his journey to become the next Godfather.

We also see a "head of the snake" application in the character of Emilio Barzini. While the Big World external conflict has a lot of bad guys, including all four heads of the rival gang families, the story consistently isolates Barzini as the leader. Other bad guys come and go, but the audience has a special relationship with Barzini and we understand that Barzini's fate represents the group.

*The Godfather* is an excellent example of using an internal conflict to drive a story. *It should be noted that this film is not recommended for family viewing.*

*The Godfather* was written by Mario Puzo.

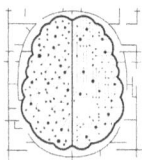

# IT'S A WONDERFUL LIFE NOVEL MATRIX WORKSHEETS

## Contents:

*It's a Wonderful Life* One Universe

*It's a Wonderful Life* Three Acts

*It's a Wonderful Life* Five Conflicts Worksheet

*It's a Wonderful Life* Seven Characters Worksheet

Find additional example plans at
**NovelMatrix.com**

# One Universe
## *It's a Wonderful Life*

| ELEMENT | WHAT'S POSSIBLE? | WHAT'S NORMAL? |
|---------|------------------|----------------|
| SOCIAL NORMS | Men and women relate to each other as social equals, but race-based social classes are still common. Colleges are gaining popularity. | While men and women relate as equals, it may lead to rumor/scandal. Most people are vocationally trained. The servant class is treated with respect and dignity. |
| MAGIC/SUPERNATURAL | God intervenes in the lives of men by sending angels to interact directly with them. | Most characters never experience angelic visitation, and are hesitant to believe any account of it. |
| PHYSICAL ACTIONS/ REACTIONS | A good punch will knock a man down and end a fight. | In the relatively polite society of 1945 New England, physical confrontations are uncommon and cause for alarm. |
| ROMANCE/LOVE | True love is meaningful and long-lasting. | Characters actively seek out marriage and consider it a lifelong commitment. Men and women kiss publicly when married or dating. |

## the novel matrix

| | | |
|---|---|---|
| **SERENDIPITY** | Incidents of serendipity are due to God interacting in the lives of men. | Most characters experience events which they would attribute to the work of God. |
| **TECHNOLOGY** | Set in the late 1940s, the technology is consistent with the actual technology of the time period. | Technology changes over the course of the movie, including the introduction of the car, which is commonplace by 1945. |
| **ANGELS** | Angels are deceased people, who are given assignments to "earn their wings." Every time a bell rings, an angel has earned its wings. | Angels are well-meaning, but may be incompetent. God defers to the decision of the assigned-angel in many cases. |
| *(ADDITIONAL ELEMENT)* | | |
| *(ADDITIONAL ELEMENT)* | | |

Highlight items that have a direct bearing on the plot and premise of your story. Specifically develop these elements early in the manuscript.

# Three-Act Structure
## *It's a Wonderful Life*

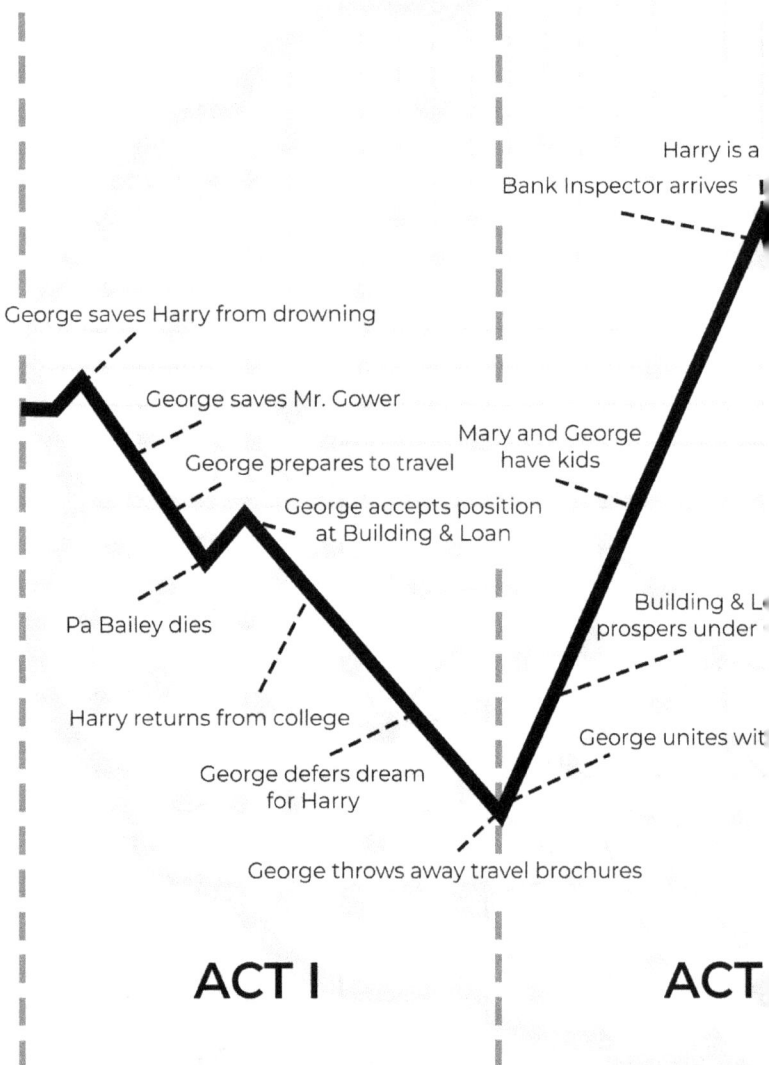

Harry is a

Bank Inspector arrives

George saves Harry from drowning

George saves Mr. Gower

George prepares to travel

Mary and George
have kids

George accepts position
at Building & Loan

Building & L
prospers under

Pa Bailey dies

Harry returns from college

George unites wit

George defers dream
for Harry

George throws away travel brochures

**ACT I**

**ACT**

How is the protagonist trapped
(without agency)?

George is too good.
He will always put everyone else first.

# the novel matrix

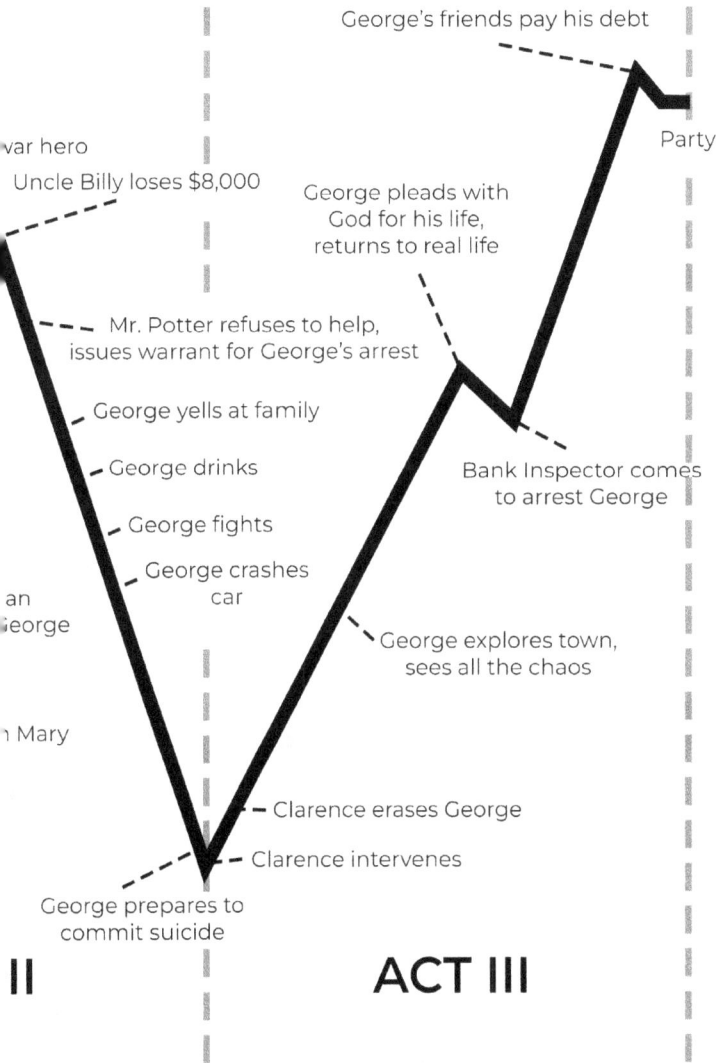

George's friends pay his debt

var hero

Uncle Billy loses $8,000

Party

George pleads with
God for his life,
returns to real life

Mr. Potter refuses to help,
issues warrant for George's arrest

George yells at family

George drinks

Bank Inspector comes
to arrest George

George fights

George crashes
car

an
George

George explores town,
sees all the chaos

Mary

Clarence erases George

Clarence intervenes

George prepares to
commit suicide

II

## ACT III

What **Impossible Thing** will
the protagonist achieve?

Change his mind about success
to understand his value

# Five Conflicts

*It's a Wonderful Life*

**the novel matrix**

## Little World Conflicts

**INTERNAL**

Live a "successful" life

*vs*

Fulfill duty to community

**EXTERNAL**

George

*vs*

Bank Inspector

**PHILOSOPHICAL**

Every life has value

*vs*

A man's value is his accomplishments

## Big World Conflicts

**INTERNAL**

X

**EXTERNAL**

Family business

*vs*

Big business

**PHILOSOPHICAL**

People are success

*vs*

Profits are success

Put a square around the **Driving Conflict**.

How will the LW external conflict manifest?
Are the protagonist and antagonist in competition for the same thing, or do they have mutually exclusive goals?

> The Bank Inspector will put George in jail if he fails to correct Uncle Billy's mistake.

How will the LW internal conflict manifest?
What will happen that shows and amplifies the problem in the protagonist's heart?

> Because of George's goodness, he will lose all of his dreams and almost his life, which will force him to choose what's really important.

# Seven Characters

*It's a Wonderful Life*

**the novel matrix**

| ARCHETYPE | FUNCTION | CHARACTER |
|---|---|---|
| GUIDE | 1. EXPLAINS THE UNIVERSE<br>2. ESTABLISHES THE PROTAGONIST'S MISSION | Pa Bailey →<br>Ma Bailey →<br>Clarence |
| SIDEKICK | 1. PROVIDES TOOLS, SKILLS, AND RESOURCES<br>2. ESTABLISHES LIKEABILITY | Mary |
| FRENEMY | 1. INJECTS A VARIABLE INTO THE SCENE<br>2. MAY BE POS. OR NEG. | Uncle Billy |
| OBJECT OF AFFECTION | 1. CATALYZES THE PROTAGONIST TO ACTION<br>2. IS NEVER HELPFUL | Harry |
| ANTAGONIST | 1. DIRECTLY OPPOSES PROTAGONIST<br>2. OFTEN A VICTIM OF THE SYSTEM | Bank Inspector |
| MEGA-ANTAGONIST | 1. REPRESENTS EVERYTHING WRONG WITH THE UNIVERSE<br>2. JUST PLAIN EVIL | Mr. Potter |

REASONABLE CHARACTER COMBOS

| | GUIDE | SIDEKICK | FRENEMY | OBJECT | ANTAGONIST | MEGA-A |
|---|---|---|---|---|---|---|
| GUIDE | | | ✓ | ✓ | | |
| SIDEKICK | | | | | | |
| FRENEMY | ✓ | | | | | |
| OBJECT | ✓ | | | | ✓ | |
| ANTAGONIST | | | ✓ | | | |
| MEGA-A | | | | | | |

Which two characters will embody the LW philosophical conflict?

Clarence

George Bailey

## Notes on
# It's a Wonderful Life

Originally released in 1946, *It's a Wonderful Life* is a classic example of the principles of the Novel Matrix.

We see a classic three-act structure, with easily discernible plot points where the direction of the story changes.

In this story, it's notable that George Bailey holds one of the philosophical positions in the Little World philosophical conflict at the beginning of the story, and he primarily agrees with his Mega-Antagonist!

Rather than being caught between two philosophical positions, George begins the story entrenched in a position that's very harmful to his happiness. The opposing side of the conflict is held by almost every supporting character, but most notably by the Guide character.

Here we see a "relay" of the Guide character. The story begins with George's father, Pa Bailey, as the Guide. When he dies, Ma Bailey steps into the Guide position. As we move into the third act, Clarence becomes the Guide.

We typically only see relay characters for the Guide. It's important that the previous guide is completely eliminated from the story before a new one steps in. We never have two Guides at the same time. It's also important that everyone who fills the Guide position agrees with the other Guides. Their ideas are never in contest but are always a continuation of the same mission.

It's also notable that in this story the Mega-Antagonist gets a lot more attention than the Antagonist. While George does resolve all three Little World conflicts, the Big World remains untouched.

*It's a Wonderful Life* was based on a short story titled "The Greatest Gift" by Philip Van Doren Stern, and adapted by Frank Capra.

# GLOSSARY

The glossary includes a selection of terms that are unique to (or used uniquely within) *The Novel Matrix.*

ACT – In long-form stories, an act is a series of events that precipitatea dramatic change to the protagonist's trajectory, mission, or accomplishments.

AGENCY – A character's ability to self-determine and take action on his or her own behalf.

ANTAGONIST – A character who actively opposes the protagonist in the accomplishment of his or her mission. The antagonist may be defeated by destruction or conversion (changing sides).

BIG WORLD – The circumstances and conflicts the protagonist is a member of, which effect larger groups or populations than the protagonist and his direct relationships.

CONFLICT – Two things in tension, such that both may not be satisfied at the same time.

DRIVING CONFLICT – The most important conflict for which the reader feels an emotional burden.

DUTY TO DEVELOP BACKSTORY – The storyteller's responsibility to explain how a character has developed his or her skills, resources, relationships, and personality.

DUTY TO MAINTAIN – The storyteller's responsibility to keep the audience appraised of the status of certain elements, most notably secondary characters, subplots, and all five conflicts.

FRENEMY – A character who inconsistently brings positive and negative value to the Protagonist's journey.

INTERNAL CONFLICT – A conflict occurring inside of a character's head and heart, usually a hard decision that the character must make.

IMPOSSIBLE THING – An objective that is seemingly impossible for the protagonist at the beginning of the story.

LITTLE WORLD – The circumstances and conflicts that relate directly to the protagonist and which have little effect outside of the protagonist and his immediate relationships.

MEGA-ANTAGONIST – The primary ruler or architect of the Big World conflict. Defeating the Mega-Antagonist would result in systemic change in the universe of the story.

NARRATIVE POINT-OF-VIEW – The set of rules which determine the narrator's perspective and the limitations governing the narrator's knowledge of the universe.

OBJECT OF AFFECTION – Also referred to as "Object." A character that catalyzes the protagonist to make poor choices. Sometimes the Object of Affection is also a romantic interest, but need not be so.

PHILOSOPHICAL CONFLICT – Two worldviews in tension with each other.

PROTAGONIST – The "first hero," almost always the main character of the book. This term may be used interchangeably with hero or main character, even if this character is not "heroic" in a conventional sense.

SCENE – A complete unit of story. Usually a continuous series of actions limited to a specific time and space.

SEMI-OMNISCIENT - A narrative point-of-view in which the narrator seems to only know the internal state (thoughts, feelings, desires, etc.) of a limited number of characters—usually just one character.

SUBPLOT – A storyline that exists independently of the five conflicts.

www.ingramcontent.com/pod-product-compliance
Lightning Source LLC
Chambersburg PA
CBHW072341090426
42741CB00012B/2868

Essays on Wealth, Generosity, and Legacy